WONDERFUL WORDS OF
LIFE

WONDERFUL WORDS OF LIFE

WONDERFUL WORDS OF
LIFE

Daily Inspiration for
The GOOD LIFE

Tawanda Prince

Copyright © 2015 Tawanda Prince

Printed and bound in the United States of America. All rights reserved. No part of this book may be reproduced or transmitted in any form or by any means, electronic or mechanical, including photocopying, recording, or by an information storage or retrieval system, except by a reviewer who may quote brief passages in a review to be printed in a magazine or newspaper, without permission in writing form the publisher.

For information contact Rosie Lane Publishing, 6400 Baltimore National Pike #988, Baltimore, MD 21208.

Unless otherwise noted all scripture quotations are taken from the New King James Version®. Copyright © 1982 by Thomas Nelson, Inc. Used by permission. All rights reserved.

Scripture quotations marked (NIV) are taken from the Holy Bible, New International Version®, NIV®. Copyright © 1973, 1978, 1984, 2011 by Biblica, Inc.™ Used by permission of Zondervan. All rights reserved worldwide. www.zondervan.com The "NIV" and "New International Version" are trademarks registered in the United States Patent and Trademark Office by Biblica, Inc.™

Scripture quotations marked KJV are from the King James version.

Printed in the United States of America

19 18 17 16 15   987654321

Published by Rosie Lane Publishing

Author's website: www.Agoodlifecoach.com

ISBN: 978-0-692-35331-8

Book design: Tawanda Prince
Cover design: kkproductions.biz
Cover photographs: BIG Mike
Editor: Wendy Stevens

WONDERFUL WORDS OF LIFE

DEDICATION

This book is dedicated to the 1999 curve ball that unexpectedly came my way and propelled me into THE GOOD LIFE.

Thank you God for your "Master" plan.

WONDERFUL WORDS OF LIFE

Acknowledgements

I would like to acknowledge all those who believed in me, even when it was difficult to believe in myself. When my back was against the wall (quite often), you held me up; and when I fell, you raised me up.

A special thank you to my parents who have walked with me every step of the way. Your unending love, grace and support (including supplying another computer when my laptop blew out while in the final stages of completing this book) have been my rock. Thank you from the bottom of my grateful heart.

To my children, Javon and Sarah, who continue to give me inspiration to be and do my best, and who always believed that "I can do it". A special thanks to my daughter who provided her computer for the "in-between" time.

To my muse: you have been the perfect "knight in shining armor for this damsel in distress." Thank you for catching hold of the vision and seeing things that even I couldn't see.

To my writing sisters in the struggle…Diane, Journey, Sharon, Sheila, Jacinta, LeQuan, Sonja, Kay Renee, Melissa, Chanda, Adair and Stacy; you inspire me. WRITE ON! To my godfather Mel Branker, my first writing coach, thanks for pushing me. To my editor Wendy and her partner-in-Christ Digital Joe thanks for blessing Tyliesha…

To Dr. Abuzahra and Dr. Soodan, thanks for the "medicine".

Most importantly I want to thank God for trusting me with the gifts and talents that he has bestowed upon me and for giving me a second and third chance to use them. The Bible says, *"A man's gift makes room for him and brings him before great men."* Proverbs 18:16, and I am learning that more each day. Thank you God for allowing me to live **THE GOOD LIFE.**

WONDERFUL WORDS OF LIFE

WONDERFUL WORDS OF LIFE

Fore-WORD

Sing them over again to me
Wonderful words of life
Let me more of their beauty see
Wonderful words of life
Words of life and beauty
Teach me faith and duty
Beautiful words, wonderful words
Wonderful words of life
Beautiful words, wonderful words
Wonderful words of life

Wonderful Words of Life/Phillip P. Bliss

As a child, I can recall hearing this age-old hymn being sung by my grandmother from the pews of our church, First Congregational Church of Morrisania, Bronx, New York. She always sang this catchy tune loudly and very off key, but that helps to make it even more memorable. This is indeed one of those songs that have stuck with me over the years. However, throughout my life's journey, the song has grown to mean so much more. I have discovered that words have power, and the power of life and death are in the tongue. It is of utmost importance to speak life.

We must speak life! Speak wonderful words of life that glorify, edify and transform. Wonderful words of life that set the flow of goodness in motion. Speak wonderful

WONDERFUL WORDS OF LIFE

words that empower and align with the voice of creation to manifest your very best. Speak wonderful words that lead you to **the Good Life**.

So just what is ***"the good life"***? Simply put, it is a life that is lined up with God's master plan. It is a life that is fully surrendered to the divine life design, and open to purpose driven possibilities. ***The good life*** is a life that says yes to God and operates in agreement with the promises that God has for you. It is a life that feasts on the fruits of passion, purpose and power. It is a life without regrets; that refuses to see life's lessons as failures, but rather as opportunities for growth and even greater possibilities. ***The good life*** is not good because it is full of good ideas, but rather "God ideas" activated by faith. ***The good life*** embodies the belief that all things are possible with God.

Many people think of ***the good life*** as a life filled with all of the trappings of success. People often confuse the trophies of a good life with the blessings of ***the good life***. ***The good life*** is not based on how much you can get, do, buy or have. However when you truly live ***the good life*** according to God's master plan you open the divine pathway to do, have and be more.

Words Have Power

Words have power and you shall have what you say. Your words have the power to bring into fruition what you confess and to call into reality what you profess. If you speak doubt and negativity you bring about death, both literally and figuratively. You bring death to your bodies when you profess sickness and lay claim to defeat. Likewise, you also speak death to your dreams when you profess fear and failure. When you doubt in your mind and you seal it with your words, your proclamation determines your destination.

However, when you speak life you awaken positive possibilities. Your words align with your faith and you open up the gateway to **the good life**. Your positive words can speak goodness into existence. When you call those things that are not, as though they were; you tap into God's divine system of manifestation and actualization. You have the ability to make it rain showers of blessings just by what you say.

You must decree and declare **the good life**, no matter what your life looks like. You must apply God's truth about who you are, what you will have and what you will do. This is not to say that only good things will happen; but whatever happens, God is working it out for your good. When you speak in agreement with that, you unleash the power of heaven to yield for you **the good life.**

Speak Life

Not only do words have power but they have assignments. Words can lock you down and block you or they can release you to reach your greatest potential. When the world was created, God powerfully spoke the stars, the sea, the earth and the fullness thereof into existence. Word power is indeed divine power. ***"In the beginning was the word and the word was with God and the word was God...and the word became flesh and dwelt among us." John 1:1 & 14*** Everything that exists has come forth from words. Life sprang forth from words and all things were created from the living word. Words have power.

Speaking life is not simply what *you* say but it is speaking in agreement with what God says. When your words line up with the truth you become unstoppable, unbreakable, unshakeable and unable to fail. Therefore word power is divine power. ***"And they overcame by the blood of the lamb and the word of their testimony."*** Revelations 12:11 This assures you that your words are tied to your breakthrough. When you are "over-come" you are able to overcome by your testimony along with the divine transforming power in the blood of the lamb.

My Journey to "The Good Life"

"All things work together for good to those who love God to those who are the called according to his purpose." Romans 8:28

My road to ***the good life*** has been a path riddled with trials, troubles and triumphs. Like many, my journey to ***the good life*** did not always feel good, but ultimately it all worked together for the "good". My turning point came about when I experienced a life changing event that propelled me out of my comfort zone into God's possibility zone.

In January 1999, I suffered four heart attacks and underwent emergency quadruple bypass surgery. This unexpected life crisis opened the door for me to experience many miracles including dying twice and being brought back to life. During this process I came to experience God as a healer, restorer and not only giver of life, but the giver of ***the good life.***

My Journey has allowed me to understand what it means to truly surrender and live with a passion for purpose, ignited by God's power. I came to understand what it means to say, *"Not my will but thy will be done."* I understand that He is the only way to the good life. True fulfillment comes when you follow the path that God has for you.

Although my journey included a life changing personal crisis, it led me to see that my mission here is to help direct other people down the pathway to **the good life**. It is not enough to understand it myself, but to spread the good news that Jesus still heals, saves and delivers. I must let others know that God can turn a test into a testimony, a mess into a message and mistakes into a ministry. A break down can in fact lead to a breakthrough and what the enemy may have intended for your destruction can in fact bring your deliverance. Your pitfall can actually become your platform for positive possibilities; where broken places and pieces can lead to peace. The only way to enjoy **the good life** is to be willing to give up the comfortable life. You are given a choice and you must choose life...**the good life.**

I am living **the good life** not because I have it **"good"** all the time, but because it's all **good**. I know that I am *the called* according to his purpose and I yield to that divine purpose. Although while on this journey I have encountered many twists and turns, I know I am on the right path. ***"Let us not become weary in doing good, for at the proper time we will reap a harvest if we do not give up." Galatians 6:9 NIV***

WONDERFUL WORDS OF LIFE

Wonderful Words of Life

This book is intended to provide a daily word for your focus. It is possibly that one word that could make all the difference in your mindset, which directly affects your outcome. That one word that can be the answer to a secret that God has been longing to share with you. That one word that could be the key to your breakthrough or help you resolve an issue that you are wrestling with. That one word that can move a mountain, bring down a wall or build a bridge in your life. That one word that could lead to acceptance of a situation and bring you peace. Words like balance, power, restore, faith, grow, serve, limitless, elevate, love, unbroken and vision can bring about a breakthrough. It could be that one word that connects you to the message that God has for you; and can make all the difference in your life.

Say So...

"Let the redeemed of the Lord say so." Psalm 107:2

I have learned on this journey that I must believe, seek and speak my way to **the good life**. The power of life that is in my tongue must be engaged daily to help me to reach my God-size possibilities. Daily prayers, affirmations and declarations are empowering. My personal affirmation is, ***"I am living the good life God created me to live doing the good work God created me to do."*** This is my declaration, commitment and mission.

"Let the words of my mouth and the meditation of my heart be acceptable in thy sight, O Lord my strength and my redeemer." Psalm 19:14

Affirmations are statements that we proclaim to ourselves and others about ourselves. These positive statements of faith lead to positive actions. Affirmations repeated throughout the day remind us of our daily focus. They give us marching orders as we navigate through the daily onslaught of opposition. As we press toward *the mark of the high calling* on our lives, we are armed with powerful words that declare us victorious.

I have termed affirmations as "Life-lines". The dictionary definition of a lifeline is, "a **line used for saving and preserving life; something regarded as indispensable for the maintaining or protection of life; something which provides help or support that is needed for success or survival.**" This is precisely the function and purpose of affirmations (Life-lines) to one who is in pursuit of **the good life.** By declaring daily Life-lines you will empower yourself with wonderful words of life, and you shall have what you say.

As the hymn also reminds us:

Words so freely given

Wooing us to heaven

Beautiful words, wonderful words

Wonderful words of life

Beautiful words, wonderful words

Wonderful words of life

WONDERFUL WORDS OF LIFE

How to Use this Book

This book contains a page for each day from January through December. Each page has 3 sections: Word of the Day, Today's Life-line, and **The Good Life** Application. **The Word of the Day** is your focus word that serves as a mental compass to help point you in a positive direction. **Today's Life-line** is your daily power statement that can be used to reinforce your focus. Repeat this statement to yourself throughout the day or meditate on this as a one line prayer or weapon against negativity. **The Good Life Application** is the space allocated for your personal response. You may write your own thoughts, revelations, prayers, questions emotions, confirmations or simply just good vibrations. Additionally, each month features an introduction that reflects on a focus word for that month.

The Choice is Yours

Option 1-Reading Plan

You can choose to begin this book on January 1 of any year and read it daily through December 31. This plan is great for those who begin reading at the start of a new year.

Option 2- Reading Plan

You can choose to start on any date of the year and read through for one complete year. For example one might begin reading on May 29th and read through daily until May 28th the following year. Also, you can choose to engage in a concentrated study for 30, 60 or 90 days and begin with any day# that you choose.

Option3-Reading Plan

You can choose to start at any day of the year as day #1 and read through day #365. This plan is great for those who start at a random point during the year but wish to begin at the beginning of the book.

The choice is yours. It doesn't matter which plan you choose. What matters most is that you make a commitment to activate the powerful use of words and affirmations for living **the good life**. Allow God to speak to you through the words on these pages and you will begin to speak life and invite wonderful possibilities into your life. As you change your words, you will witness a transformation of your mind, actions and outcomes and these will truly become ***"Wonderful words of Life".***

January

VISIONARY

"Without vision the people perish." Proverbs 29:18 KJV

In order to live **the good life**, one must be a visionary. You must first capture in your mind's eye what you are called to do. You must make the divine connection; tapping into what God has called and created you to do. How sweet it is to know that you were created to fulfill the dream and vision that no one else can fill. To know that even before God spoke the world into existence; your purpose was already a part of his vision. Now, you must catch hold of that vision for yourself.

Dare to see beyond your own abilities, talents, resources, connections, boundaries and limitations. None of these really matter. What matters most is that your vision is birthed out of the "master plan". When you place your vision in the Master's hand, the sky is the limit.

So if you want to live **the good life**, you must dare to dream...and DREAM BIG!

D-Determined to make it happen

R-Resourceful using all things available

E-Excited and on fire in anticipation

A-Armed and prepared for whatever happens

M-Motivated by your mission

B-Believing

I-in

G-God

      For the one who has vision and dares to **DREAM BIG** is the one who is sure to live ***the good life***.

WONDERFUL WORDS OF LIFE

Day 1   **January 1**

The word of the day is...
VISION

Today's Life-line
Today I will write my VISION and make it plain.

The Good Life Application

_____

_____

_____

_____

_____

WONDERFUL WORDS OF LIFE

Day 2 　　　　　　　　**January 2**

The word of the day is...
ELEVATE

Today's Life-line

Today I ELEVATE my thinking to another level so that I may live THE GOOD LIFE.

The Good Life Application

_____

_____

_____

_____

_____

Day 3   **January 3**

The word of the day is…
WONDERFUL

Today's Life-line

Today I speak beautiful and WONDERFUL words of life.

The Good Life Application

_____

_____

_____

_____

_____

WONDERFUL WORDS OF LIFE

Day 4   **January 4**

The word of the day is…
ORDER

Today's Life-line
Today I operate in divine ORDER.

The Good Life Application

_____

_____

_____

_____

_____

WONDERFUL WORDS OF LIFE

Day 5   **January 5**

The word of the day is...
BALANCE

Today's Life-line

Today I strive to BALANCE all dimensions of my life.

The Good Life Application

_____

_____

_____

_____

_____

WONDERFUL WORDS OF LIFE

Day 6   **January 6**

The word of the day is…

THANKS

Today's Life-line

Today I give THANKS for all of my blessings.

The Good Life Application

_____

_____

_____

_____

_____

Day 7   **January 7**

The word of the day is...

TRUST

Today's Life-line

Today I TRUST in the Lord and lean not to my own understanding.

The Good Life Application

_____

_____

_____

_____

_____

WONDERFUL WORDS OF LIFE

Day 8   **January 8**

The word of the day is…
PRAISE

Today's Life-line
Today I PRAISE God unashamedly.

The Good Life Application

_____

_____

_____

_____

_____

Day 9   **January 9**

The word of the day is...

BREAKTHROUGH

Today's Life-line

Today I look with expectation for my BREAKTHROUGH.

The Good Life Application

_____

_____

_____

_____

_____

WONDERFUL WORDS OF LIFE

Day 10   **January 10**

The word of the day is…
RELEASE

Today's Life-line
Today I RELEASE toxic people and situations.

The Good Life Application

_____

_____

_____

_____

_____

WONDERFUL WORDS OF LIFE

Day 11   **January 11**

The word of the day is...
GIVE

Today's Life-line
Today I GIVE 100% of myself.

The Good Life Application

_____

_____

_____

_____

_____

WONDERFUL WORDS OF LIFE

Day 12 **January 12**

The word of the day is…

MULTIPLY

Today's Life-line

Today I give and my blessings MULTIPLY.

The Good Life Application

_____

_____

_____

_____

_____

WONDERFUL WORDS OF LIFE

Day 13   **January 13**

The word of the day is…

MORE

Today's Life-line

Today I give MORE, do MORE and become MORE.

The Good Life Application

_____

_____

_____

_____

_____

WONDERFUL WORDS OF LIFE

Day 14   January 14

The word of the day is...
STAND

Today's Life-line
Today I STAND in agreement and unity with someone else.

The Good Life Application

_____

_____

_____

_____

_____

Day 15   **January 15**

The word of the day is...

REACH

Today's Life-line

Today I allow God to use me to REACH others.

The Good Life Application

_____

_____

_____

_____

_____

WONDERFUL WORDS OF LIFE

Day 16   **January 16**

The word of the day is…

THINK

Today's Life-line

Today I THINK before I speak.

The Good Life Application

_____

_____

_____

_____

_____

Day 17　　　　　　　**January 17**

The word of the day is…

STUDY

Today's Life-line

Today I STUDY God's word for food to nourish my spirit.

The Good Life Application

_____

_____

_____

_____

_____

WONDERFUL WORDS OF LIFE

Day 18 **January 18**

The word of the day is...
MOVE

Today's Life-line

Today I MOVE according to God's master plan that leads me to THE GOOD LIFE.

The Good Life Application

_____

_____

_____

_____

_____

WONDERFUL WORDS OF LIFE

Day 19   **January 19**

The word of the day is...
PEACE

Today's Life-line

Today I give up my right to be right, for the sake of PEACE.

The Good Life Application

_____

_____

_____

_____

_____

WONDERFUL WORDS OF LIFE

Day 20   **January 20**

The word of the day is...

SOAR

Today's Life-line

Today I SOAR in the realm of THE GOOD LIFE possibilities.

The Good Life Application

_____

_____

_____

_____

WONDERFUL WORDS OF LIFE

Day 21 **January 21**

The word of the day is...
PRAY

Today's Life-line
Today I PRAY without ceasing.

The Good Life Application

_____

_____

_____

_____

_____

WONDERFUL WORDS OF LIFE

Day 22   **January 22**

The word of the day is...

REJOICE

Today's Life-line

Today I REJOICE with others who are rejoicing about their blessings.

The Good Life Application

_____

_____

_____

_____

_____

WONDERFUL WORDS OF LIFE

Day 23   **January 23**

The word of the day is...
HELP

Today's Life-line
Today I offer or ask for HELP.

The Good Life Application

_____

_____

_____

_____

_____

WONDERFUL WORDS OF LIFE

Day 24   **January 24**

The word of the day is…
SERVE

Today's Life-line
Today I gladly SERVE God and others.

The Good Life Application

_____

_____

_____

_____

_____

Day 25   **January 25**

The word of the day is...

STRETCH

Today's Life-line

Today I STRETCH beyond my self-imposed borders.

The Good Life Application

_____

_____

_____

_____

_____

WONDERFUL WORDS OF LIFE

Day 26   **January 26**

The word of the day is...
WAIT

Today's Life-line
Today I WAIT...*patiently*.

The Good Life Application

_____

_____

_____

_____

_____

WONDERFUL WORDS OF LIFE

Day 27 **January 27**

The word of the day is...
BELIEVE

Today's Life-line
Today I BELIEVE that I will live THE GOOD LIFE.

The Good Life Application

_____

_____

_____

_____

_____

Day 28   **January 28**

The word of the day is…

PURSUE

Today's Life-line

Today I PURSUE the things of God.

The Good Life Application

_____

_____

_____

_____

_____

Day 29   **January 29**

The word of the day is…

FAITH

Today's Life-line

Today I use my FAITH to move mountains.

The Good Life Application

_____

_____

_____

_____

_____

WONDERFUL WORDS OF LIFE

Day 30   **January 30**

The word of the day is…

PROVISION

Today's Life-line

Today I rely on God for PROVISION for the vision.

The Good Life Application

_____

_____

_____

_____

_____

Day 31   January 31

The word of the day is...
RENEW

Today's Life-line
Today I RENEW my sense of purpose.

The Good Life Application

_____

_____

_____

_____

_____

WONDERFUL WORDS OF LIFE

February

STRENGTH

"The joy of the Lord is your strength." Nehemiah 8:10

In order to live **the good life**, you will need strength for the journey. Yes, your journey will be full of hills, mountains, valleys and bridges to cross. However, you are never left alone to rely on your own limited strength; through God you have access to an endless supply of strength and resilience. ***"My strength is made perfect in weakness." 2 Corinthians 12:9***

When you learn to take cover under the almighty wings, you will find joy. There is a joy that comes from knowing that where God leads, he feeds; where God gives vision, he gives provision; and you can do all things through Christ who gives you strength. When you truly find this joy that the world can't take away you are empowered with divine strength.

Divine strength helps you overcome obstacles, and withstand disappointments. Divine strength empowers you to believe in a positive outcome even in the face of trials. This strength causes you to be like a tree planted by the rivers of waters as your very soul declares, *"I shall not be moved."*

Furthermore, God is delighted when you delight in him. When you take joy in him he blesses you beyond your dreams to live **the good life**. These blessings are not merely to have more "stuff", but to make more of a difference in the world as you were created to do.

"The Lord God is my strength. He will make my feet like deer's feet and will make me walk on high places."
Habakkuk 3:19

Day 32   February 1

The word of the day is…

STRENGTH

Today's Life-line

Today I tap into God's wellspring of joy for my strength.

The Good Life Application

_____

_____

_____

_____

_____

Day 33   February 2

The word of the day is…
OBEDIENT

Today's Life-line
Today I am OBEDIENT to God's will.

The Good Life Application

_____

_____

_____

_____

_____

WONDERFUL WORDS OF LIFE

Day 34   February 3

The word of the day is…

INTEGRITY

Today's Life-line

Today I show INTEGRITY through my words, thoughts and actions.

The Good Life Application

_____

_____

_____

_____

_____

Day 35   **February 4**

The word of the day is…

WISDOM

Today's Life-line

Today I apply WISDOM in every situation that I face.

The Good Life Application

_____

_____

_____

_____

_____

Day 36   February 5

The word of the day is…

GLORIFY

Today's Life-line

Today I GLORIFY God by reflecting his light.

The Good Life Application

_____

_____

_____

_____

_____

WONDERFUL WORDS OF LIFE

Day 37 **February 6**

The word of the day is...

JUSTIFIED

Today's Life-line

Today I am thankful that I am JUSTIFIED through God's grace.

The Good Life Application

_____

_____

_____

_____

_____

Day 38   February 7

The word of the day is…

PURE

Today's Life-line
Today I keep my heart and life PURE.

The Good Life Application

_____

_____

_____

_____

_____

Day 39 **February 8**

The word of the day is…

HOLINESS

Today's Life-line

Today I strive for HOLINESS in all that I say and do.

The Good Life Application

_____

_____

_____

_____

_____

WONDERFUL WORDS OF LIFE

Day 40   **February 9**

The word of the day is...

SACRIFICE

Today's Life-line

Today I SACRIFICE something that is comfortable now so that I can live THE GOOD LIFE later.

The Good Life Application

_____

_____

_____

_____

_____

WONDERFUL WORDS OF LIFE

Day 41   **February 10**

The word of the day is…

HONESTY

Today's Life-line

Today I speak with HONESTY and tell the truth with love.

The Good Life Application

_____

_____

_____

_____

_____

WONDERFUL WORDS OF LIFE

Day 42　　　　　　　　　February 11

The word of the day is…
BOLD

Today's Life-line
Today I am BOLD in my pursuit of THE GOOD LIFE.

The Good Life Application

_____

_____

_____

_____

_____

WONDERFUL WORDS OF LIFE

Day 43 **February 12**

The word of the day is...
SANCTIFIED

Today's Life-line

Today I thank God that I am SANCTIFIED and set apart for his high and holy purpose.

The Good Life Application

_____

_____

_____

_____

_____

WONDERFUL WORDS OF LIFE

Day 44   **February 13**

The word of the day is...

ENDURE

Today's Life-line

Today I rely on God to help me to ENDURE all things.

The Good Life Application

_____

_____

_____

_____

_____

WONDERFUL WORDS OF LIFE

Day 45   **February 14**

The word of the day is…

LOVE

Today's Life-line

Today I give and receive LOVE.

The Good Life Application

_____

_____

_____

_____

_____

Day 46   **February 15**

The word of the day is…
RIGHTEOUS

Today's Life-line

Today I am empowered with RIGHTEOUS indignation against those who oppress others.

The Good Life Application

_____

_____

_____

_____

_____

WONDERFUL WORDS OF LIFE

Day 47   February 16

The word of the day is…
DO

Today's Life-line
Today I will DO whatever God says.

The Good Life Application

_____

_____

_____

_____

_____

WONDERFUL WORDS OF LIFE

Day 48   **February 17**

The word of the day is…

OFFER

Today's Life-line

Today I OFFER something I have to share with someone in need.

The Good Life Application

_____

_____

_____

_____

_____

Day 49   **February 18**

The word of the day is...
WORSHIP

Today's Life-line
Today I WORSHIP God in spirit and in truth.

The Good Life Application

_____

_____

_____

_____

_____

WONDERFUL WORDS OF LIFE

Day 50   February 19

The word of the day is...
MAGNIFY

Today's Life-line
Today I MAGNIFY my God, not my problems.

The Good Life Application

_____

_____

_____

_____

_____

WONDERFUL WORDS OF LIFE

Day 51   **February 20**

The word of the day is…
LEAD

Today's Life-line
Today I LEAD those assigned to me with love.

The Good Life Application

_____

_____

_____

_____

_____

WONDERFUL WORDS OF LIFE

Day 52   February 21

The word of the day is...

BUILD

Today's Life-line

Today I BUILD my future on a solid foundation.

The Good Life Application

_____

_____

_____

_____

_____

Day 53   **February 22**

The word of the day is...

REBUILD

Today's Life-line

Today I REBUILD that which has been torn down.

The Good Life Application

_____

_____

_____

_____

_____

WONDERFUL WORDS OF LIFE

Day 54   **February 23**

The word of the day is…

SHARE

Today's Life-line

Today I SHARE all, not just my overflow.

The Good Life Application

_____

_____

_____

_____

_____

WONDERFUL WORDS OF LIFE

Day 55   **February 24**

The word of the day is…

CARE

Today's Life-line

Today I will show others that I CARE.

The Good Life Application

_____

_____

_____

_____

_____

WONDERFUL WORDS OF LIFE

Day 56   **February 25**

The word of the day is...

HEART

Today's Life-line

Today my HEART openly reflects God's love.

The Good Life Application

_____

_____

_____

_____

_____

WONDERFUL WORDS OF LIFE

Day 57   February 26

The word of the day is...

PRAYER

Today's Life-line

Today I tap into the divine power of PRAYER to handle my life situations.

The Good Life Application

_____

_____

_____

_____

_____

Day 58   **February 27**

The word of the day is...
COVERED

Today's Life-line
Today I am COVERED by God.

The Good Life Application

_____

_____

_____

_____

_____

Day 59   **February 28**

The word of the day is…

KEPT

Today's Life-line

Today I am KEPT by God, the ultimate keeper.

The Good Life Application

_____

_____

_____

_____

_____

WONDERFUL WORDS OF LIFE

Leap Year　　　　　February 29

The word of the day is...

EXTRA

Today's Life-line

Today I go the EXTRA mile to live THE GOOD LIFE.

The Good Life Application

_____

_____

_____

_____

_____

WONDERFUL WORDS OF LIFE

March

COMMIT

"Commit to the Lord whatever you do and your plans will succeed." Proverbs 16:13 NIV

In order to live **the good life**, you must be committed. This commitment is three fold. First, you must commit yourself. It is important to know that your life is not your own because you were bought with a price. You must be committed to the one who created you and paid the price for your sins **(see Appendix A).** When you are committed to him, he leads you in the way you should go. Commitment brings contentment.

Secondly, you must commit your ways unto the Lord. That is, in order to live **the good life**, you must strive to be more like him. Your "ways" should reflect the light. Your thoughts, your words, your ideas and your pursuits must be rooted in your commitment to walk in his way. *"This is the way and walk ye in it." Isaiah 30:21 KJV*

Thirdly, in order to live **the good life**, you must commit your works unto the Lord. Everything you do must be a "God idea", not merely just a good idea. One God idea is better than ten good ideas because there is a blessing attached to it solely for you. In order for your plans to succeed they must be divine purpose driven plans. Commitment requires faith that no matter what comes your way, you are fully vested.

The good life is lived from the inside out; not the outside in. When your ways and works are committed internally, then the things that you desire externally will fall into place. Commitment requires trust in God and reckless abandon to the process that he is taking you through. When you have committed to the Lord whatever it takes to live *the good life* then your plans will succeed.

Day 60 　　　　　　　**March 1**

The word of the day is…
COMMIT

Today's Life-line

Today I COMMIT to follow my chosen path to THE GOOD LIFE.

The Good Life Application

_____

_____

_____

_____

_____

Day 61   **March 2**

The word of the day is…

GRACE

Today's Life-line

Today I extend GRACE to all.

The Good Life Application

_____

_____

_____

_____

_____

WONDERFUL WORDS OF LIFE

Day 62   March 3

The word of the day is…

SING

Today's Life-line

Today I SING in my own key of life.

The Good Life Application

_____

_____

_____

_____

_____

WONDERFUL WORDS OF LIFE

Day 63   **March 4**

The word of the day is…

DANCE

Today's Life-line

Today I DANCE to the rhythm God plays for me.

The Good Life Application

_____

_____

_____

_____

_____

Day 64   **March 5**

The word of the day is…

REFLECT

Today's Life-line

Today I REFLECT on my challenges, triumphs and blessings.

The Good Life Application

_____

_____

_____

_____

_____

WONDERFUL WORDS OF LIFE

Day 65   **March 6**

The word of the day is...

GIFTS

Today's Life-line

Today I offer my gifts and talents for God's designated use.

The Good Life Application

_____

_____

_____

_____

_____

WONDERFUL WORDS OF LIFE

Day 66   **March 7**

The word of the day is...
WHOLENESS

Today's Life-line
Today I strive to achieve wholeness.

The Good Life Application

_____

_____

_____

_____

_____

WONDERFUL WORDS OF LIFE

Day 67   **March 8**

The word of the day is…

ENCOURAGED

Today's Life-line

Today I am ENCOURAGED no matter how things look at the moment.

The Good Life Application

_____

_____

_____

_____

_____

WONDERFUL WORDS OF LIFE

Day 68   **March 9**

The word of the day is...

CHOOSE

Today's Life-line

Today I CHOOSE to do the right thing.

The Good Life Application

_____

_____

_____

_____

_____

WONDERFUL WORDS OF LIFE

Day 69   March 10

The word of the day is…
RELIEF

Today's Life-line

Today I look for God's RELIEF from all of my troubles.

The Good Life Application

_____

_____

_____

_____

_____

WONDERFUL WORDS OF LIFE

Day 70   **March 11**

The word of the day is...

CHANGE

Today's Life-line

Today I welcome and embrace the winds of CHANGE that are blowing in my life.

The Good Life Application

_____

_____

_____

_____

_____

WONDERFUL WORDS OF LIFE

Day 71   March 12

The word of the day is...
STAND

Today's Life-line
Today I STAND unmovable and unshaken.

The Good Life Application

_____

_____

_____

_____

_____

WONDERFUL WORDS OF LIFE

Day 72   March 13

The word of the day is…
SUBMIT

Today's Life-line

Today I SUBMIT my will to God's master plan for living THE GOOD LIFE.

The Good Life Application

_____

_____

_____

_____

_____

WONDERFUL WORDS OF LIFE

Day 73   March 14

The word of the day is…

FOLLOW

Today's Life-line

Today I FOLLOW my heart, which is guided by God.

The Good Life Application

_____

_____

_____

_____

_____

Day 74   **March 15**

The word of the day is…

FLOW

Today's Life-line

Today I praise God for the blessings that FLOW.

The Good Life Application

_____

_____

_____

_____

_____

WONDERFUL WORDS OF LIFE

Day 75   March 16

The word of the day is…

FORGIVE

Today's Life-line

Today I freely FORGIVE myself and others; taking no offense.

The Good Life Application

_____

_____

_____

_____

_____

Day 76 　　　　　　　　March 17

The word of the day is…

BEST

Today's Life-line
Today I offer God my BEST.

The Good Life Application

_____

_____

_____

_____

_____

Day 77　　　　March 18

The word of the day is...

SHAPING

Today's Life-line

Today I am excited about how God is SHAPING my life.

The Good Life Application

_____

_____

_____

_____

_____

Day 78   March 19

The word of the day is…

OVERCOME

Today's Life-line

Today I believe I will OVERCOME all of my challenges.

The Good Life Application

_____

_____

_____

_____

_____

WONDERFUL WORDS OF LIFE

Day 79 **March 20**

The word of the day is…

WALK

Today's Life-line

Today I WALK with divine purpose.

The Good Life Application

_____

_____

_____

_____

_____

WONDERFUL WORDS OF LIFE

Day 80   **March 21**

The word of the day is…

RISE

Today's Life-line

Today I RISE up to where God has called me.

The Good Life Application

_____

_____

_____

_____

_____

Day 81　　　　　　　　**March 22**

The word of the day is...
PERSEVERE

Today's Life-line

Today I PERSEVERE without giving in to discouragement.

The Good Life Application

_____

_____

_____

_____

_____

WONDERFUL WORDS OF LIFE

Day 82   March 23

The word of the day is…
PRESENCE

Today's Life-line

Today I bask in God's PRESENCE where there is fullness of joy.

The Good Life Application

_____

_____

_____

_____

_____

WONDERFUL WORDS OF LIFE

Day 83   March 24

The word of the day is…
PERFECTING

Today's Life-line

Today I am patient with myself while God is PERFECTING me.

The Good Life Application

_____

_____

_____

_____

_____

Day 84   **March 25**

The word of the day is...

UPRIGHT

Today's Life-line

Today I walk UPRIGHT on the path that leads me to THE GOOD LIFE.

The Good Life Application

_____

_____

_____

_____

_____

WONDERFUL WORDS OF LIFE

Day 85   **March 26**

The word of the day is...
SUPPORT

Today's Life-line
Today I offer SUPPORT to someone.

The Good Life Application

_____

_____

_____

_____

_____

WONDERFUL WORDS OF LIFE

Day 86   March 27

The word of the day is...

REFLECT

Today's Life-line

Today I REFLECT on the lessons from the past as I move toward THE GOOD LIFE.

The Good Life Application

_____

_____

_____

_____

_____

WONDERFUL WORDS OF LIFE

Day 87   March 28

The word of the day is…
INSIGHT

Today's Life-line

Today I have clear INSIGHT into a brighter future.

The Good Life Application

_____

_____

_____

_____

_____

Day 88   **March 29**

The word of the day is…
GRATITUDE

Today's Life-line
Today I express an attitude of GRATITUDE.

The Good Life Application

_____

_____

_____

_____

_____

WONDERFUL WORDS OF LIFE

Day 89   March 30

The word of the day is…

INSPIRED

Today's Life-line

Today I am INSPIRED to do whatever it takes to live THE GOOD LIFE.

The Good Life Application

_____

_____

_____

_____

_____

Day 90	March 31

The word of the day is…

EMBRACE

Today's Life-line

Today I EMBRACE the truth of who God is and who I am.

The Good Life Application

_____

_____

_____

_____

_____

WONDERFUL WORDS OF LIFE

April

WISE

"Happy is the man that finds wisdom, and the man that gets understanding. For her proceeds are better than the profits of silver and her gain than fine gold." Proverbs 3: 13-14

Wisdom is often regarded as greater than silver and gold. For within wisdom all things are contained. In order to live **the good life**, you must make wise choices. Every day our brains must navigate through a sea of choices which are influenced by our thoughts, feelings, desires, needs, emotions, urges, pleasures, pain, passion, purpose, expectations, fears, fantasies, curiosities, affections, afflictions, experiences and beliefs.

There are four keys to making wise choices:

1. *Pray and consult God regarding all areas of your life*. Allow him to guide you in the way you should go. **"Trust in the Lord with all your heart and lean not to your own understanding. In all your ways acknowledge him and he shall direct your path." Proverbs 3: 5-6**
2. *Gain understanding from the Lord*. Also, make sure you know all that you need to know regarding the choice that is at hand. **"In all your getting; get understanding." Proverbs 4:7**
3. *Avoid bad advice*. Be careful who you seek out for help. **"Blessed is the man who walks not in the counsel of the ungodly..." Psalm 1:1**

4. *Count the cost.* Think about the outcome and what you stand to gain or lose by the choice you are making. ***"For which of you, intending to build a tower, does not sit down first and count the cost?" Luke 14:28***

We are not expected to have all of the answers; but we are expected to turn to the one who does. We can live **the good life** when we allow wisdom to guide us and find peace in knowing that God is directing our path. Wisdom comes in lessons learned either through teaching or testimony. Choose wisely!

Day 91   **April 1**

The word of the day is...

WISE

Today's Life-line

Today I make WISE choices instead of taking chances.

The Good Life Application

_____

_____

_____

_____

_____

Day 92   **April 2**

The word of the day is...
DREAM

Today's Life-line
Today I will DREAM big.

The Good Life Application

_____

_____

_____

_____

_____

WONDERFUL WORDS OF LIFE

Day 93   **April 3**

The word of the day is…
HOPE

Today's Life-line
Today I keep HOPE alive.

The Good Life Application

_____

_____

_____

_____

_____

WONDERFUL WORDS OF LIFE

Day 94   April 4

The word of the day is…

LIGHT

Today's Life-line

Today I let my inner LIGHT shine.

The Good Life Application

_____

_____

_____

_____

_____

WONDERFUL WORDS OF LIFE

Day 95 April 5

The word of the day is…

CLEANSE

Today's Life-line

Today I CLEANSE my heart, mind and spirit.

The Good Life Application

_____

_____

_____

_____

_____

Day 96   **April 6**

The word of the day is…

TEACH

Today's Life-line

Today I TEACH by sharing my knowledge with others.

The Good Life Application

_____

_____

_____

_____

_____

Day 97   April 7

The word of the day is...
LEARN

Today's Life-line
Today I strive to LEARN something new.

The Good Life Application

_____

_____

_____

_____

_____

WONDERFUL WORDS OF LIFE

Day 98   **April 8**

The word of the day is…

PROSPER

Today's Life-line

Today I PROSPER in mind, body and soul.

The Good Life Application

_____

_____

_____

_____

_____

Day 99 **April 9**

The word of the day is...
SOW

Today's Life-line

Today I SOW my time, talent, or resources to help others live THE GOOD LIFE.

The Good Life Application

_____

_____

_____

_____

_____

Day 100   **April 10**

The word of the day is…

SAVE

Today's Life-line

Today I am grateful that Christ died to SAVE me.

The Good Life Application

_____

_____

_____

_____

_____

WONDERFUL WORDS OF LIFE

Day 101 April 11

The word of the day is...

JOY

Today's Life-line

Today I thank God for unspeakable JOY.

The Good Life Application

_____

_____

_____

_____

_____

WONDERFUL WORDS OF LIFE

Day 102　　　　　　　　**April 12**

The word of the day is...

WORK

Today's Life-line

Today my WORK is in line with my goals.

The Good Life Application

_____

_____

_____

_____

_____

WONDERFUL WORDS OF LIFE

Day 103   April 13

The word of the day is…

RESTORATION

Today's Life-line

Today I take steps toward RESTORATION and reconciliation.

The Good Life Application

_____

_____

_____

_____

_____

WONDERFUL WORDS OF LIFE

Day 104   April 14

The word of the day is…

UNCOMMON

Today's Life-line

Today because I dare to be UNCOMMON, I will receive UNCOMMON favor and blessings.

The Good Life Application

_____

_____

_____

_____

_____

Day 105   April 15

The word of the day is…

THROUGH

Today's Life-line

Today I confidently face each obstacle knowing that God will see me THROUGH.

The Good Life Application

_____

_____

_____

_____

_____

Day 106   April 16

The word of the day is...

CONTENT

Today's Life-line

Today I am CONTENT that I am exactly where God wants me to be.

The Good Life Application

_____

_____

_____

_____

_____

Day 107   April 17

The word of the day is…

MOBILIZE

Today's Life-line

Today I MOBILIZE my strategy to live THE GOOD LIFE.

The Good Life Application

_____

_____

_____

_____

_____

WONDERFUL WORDS OF LIFE

Day 108 April 18

The word of the day is…
TIMING

Today's Life-line
Today I operate in divine TIMING and order.

The Good Life Application

_____

_____

_____

_____

_____

| Day 109 | April 19 |

The word of the day is…

EXPAND

Today's Life-line

Today I EXPAND my vision outside of the box.

The Good Life Application

_____

_____

_____

_____

_____

Day 110   April 20

The word of the day is...

SECURE

Today's Life-line

Today I am SECURE in who God created me to be.

The Good Life Application

_____

_____

_____

_____

_____

Day 111 April 21

The word of the day is…

DESTINY

Today's Life-line
Today I am joyful about my DESTINY.

The Good Life Application

_____

_____

_____

_____

_____

Day 112   **April 22**

The word of the day is…

ABIDE

Today's Life-line

Today I ABIDE under the shadow of the almighty.

The Good Life Application

_____

_____

_____

_____

_____

WONDERFUL WORDS OF LIFE

Day 113 April 23

The word of the day is…

HONOR

Today's Life-line
Today I HONOR my word.

The Good Life Application

_____

_____

_____

_____

_____

WONDERFUL WORDS OF LIFE

Day 114   April 24

The word of the day is…

BLESSING

Today's Life-line

Today I will be an unexpected BLESSING to someone.

The Good Life Application

_____

_____

_____

_____

_____

WONDERFUL WORDS OF LIFE

Day 115   **April 25**

The word of the day is…
WORTHY

Today's Life-line
Today I walk WORTHY of my calling.

The Good Life Application

_____

_____

_____

_____

_____

Day 116   April 26

The word of the day is...
WATCH

Today's Life-line

Today I WATCH, pray and wait with joyful expectation.

The Good Life Application

_____

_____

_____

_____

_____

Day 117   April 27

The word of the day is…

REVIVE

Today's Life-line

Today I REVIVE my hopes and dreams.

The Good Life Application

_____

_____

_____

_____

_____

WONDERFUL WORDS OF LIFE

Day 118   **April 28**

The word of the day is…

LIFE

Today's Life-line

Today I am open to God's plan for my LIFE.

The Good Life Application

_____

_____

_____

_____

_____

WONDERFUL WORDS OF LIFE

Day 119   April 29

The word of the day is...

POSSIBILITIES

Today's Life-line

Today I am excited about the endless POSSIBILITIES of THE GOOD LIFE.

The Good Life Application

_____

_____

_____

_____

WONDERFUL WORDS OF LIFE

Day 120   **April 30**

The word of the day is…
SENSITIVE

Today's Life-line

Today I am SENSITIVE and responsive to the needs of others.

The Good Life Application

_____

_____

_____

_____

_____

WONDERFUL WORDS OF LIFE

May

STEWARD

"Having the gifts differing according to the grace that is given to us, let us use them." Romans 12:6

In order to live **the good life**, you must be a good steward. A steward is one who manages, or oversees people, places or things. Likewise, God expects us to be good brokers or managers of all that we have been gifted.

In your pursuit of **the good life**, there are three ways to handle your business effectively. First, you must *"handle with care."* Just like any precious or even fragile package, the things entrusted to you by God must be cared for properly. All of your "gifts" including your talents, assignments, words, appointments and anointing must be used in the manner for which it was intended to be used. The bible tells us that ***"the gifts and the calling of God are irrevocable" Romans 11:29*** but the misuse or poor stewardship may result in the derailment of your purpose and possibly death of you or your dreams.

Secondly, you must *"handle with prayer"*. You cannot truly live **the good life** without prayer. It is this open communication with God that covers you and the things that you pursue. Prayer provides clarity on your mission and helps you to be a better steward. You become a better steward when you continuously tap into the unending power source through prayer and with thanksgiving. ***"Be anxious for nothing, but in everything by prayer and supplication, with thanksgiving, let your requests be made known to God." Philippians 4:6***

Thirdly, you must *"handle with dare"*. As a good steward of the gifts that God has given you, dare to dream; dare to be bold and step out on faith. Dare to look the enemy in the face and say, **"If God is for me who can be against me" Romans 8:31**. Dare to move toward your goal using your gifts, talents and resources to yield a positive dividend. Dare to trust God and keep him at his word. Dare to have enough faith to speak to the mountain and see it move. Dare to live **the good life** and use your gifts in such a way that God will bless you with more. **"Well done thy good and faithful servant. You have been faithful over few things, I will make you ruler over many things." Matthew 25:21 KJV**

You must remember that the gifts that you possess were hand-picked by God just for you. Use your gifts wisely and do not squander them in wrongful pursuits. If you are not clear on your gifts you may need a life coach. A life coach can help you:

- Identify personal and professional goals
- Tap into your spiritual gifts and purpose
- Prepare you to pursue your mission
- Challenge unproductive mindsets, beliefs and behaviors
- Develop an action plan for success

The good life will only manifest when you do the right things and handle your business in the right way. If you want more information visit www.Agoodlifecoach.com.

Day 121   **May 1**

The word of the day is...

STEWARD

Today's Life-line

Today I am a good STEWARD over my time, talent and resources.

The Good Life Application

_____

_____

_____

_____

_____

WONDERFUL WORDS OF LIFE

Day 122   May 2

The word of the day is…

FRUITFUL

Today's Life-line

Today the work of my hands is FRUITFUL.

The Good Life Application

_____

_____

_____

_____

_____

Day 123				May 3

The word of the day is...
CONFIDENCE

Today's Life-line

Today I put no CONFIDENCE in man; but in God alone.

The Good Life Application

_____

_____

_____

_____

_____

Day 124   **May 4**

The word of the day is…
RETURN

Today's Life-line

Today I RETURN my affections to God; the one who first loved me.

The Good Life Application

_____

_____

_____

_____

_____

WONDERFUL WORDS OF LIFE

Day 125   May 5

The word of the day is…
DELIVERANCE

Today's Life-line

Today my DELIVERANCE will be a testimony to encourage someone else.

The Good Life Application

_____

_____

_____

_____

_____

Day 126   **May 6**

The word of the day is…
RECONCILLIATION

Today's Life-line

Today I make RECONCILLIATION a priority in damaged relationships.

The Good Life Application

_____

_____

_____

_____

_____

Day 127   May 7

The word of the day is…
SAFETY

Today's Life-line
Today I find SAFETY by abiding in the will of God.

The Good Life Application

_____

_____

_____

_____

_____

WONDERFUL WORDS OF LIFE

Day 128   May 8

The word of the day is...

ZEAL

Today's Life-line

Today I am fired up with ZEAL for living THE GOOD LIFE.

The Good Life Application

_____

_____

_____

_____

_____

Day 129 May 9

The word of the day is…

EXPECTANCY

Today's Life-line

Today I look ahead with an EXPECTANCY of great things to come.

The Good Life Application

_____

_____

_____

_____

_____

Day 130   May 10

The word of the day is...
SALVATION

Today's Life-line

Today I am grateful for the gift of SALVATION.
(See appendix A)

The Good Life Application

_____

_____

_____

_____

_____

Day 131   May 11

The word of the day is...

SERENITY

Today's Life-line

Today I have the SERENITY to accept the things and people that I cannot change.

The Good Life Application

_____

_____

_____

_____

_____

Day 132   May 12

The word of the day is…
GOAL

Today's Life-line

Today I press towards the completion of my GOAL.

The Good Life Application

_____

_____

_____

_____

_____

Day 133   May 13

The word of the day is…
HEAR

Today's Life-line
Today I listen closely and HEAR with my heart.

The Good Life Application

_____

_____

_____

_____

_____

Day 134   May 14

The word of the day is...
KNOWLEDGE

Today's Life-line
Today I apply and share KNOWLEDGE.

The Good Life Application

_____

_____

_____

_____

_____

WONDERFUL WORDS OF LIFE

Day 135　　　　　　　　May 15

The word of the day is...
THIRST

Today's Life-line

Today I THIRST for God to fill my cup to overflowing.

The Good Life Application

_____

_____

_____

_____

_____

Day 136   **May 16**

The word of the day is...
HUNGER

Today's Life-line
Today I HUNGER for spiritual fulfillment.

The Good Life Application

_____

_____

_____

_____

_____

Day 137   May 17

The word of the day is…

CALLING

Today's Life-line

Today I accept and pursue my divine CALLING with gladness.

The Good Life Application

_____

_____

_____

_____

_____

Day 138					May 18

The word of the day is…

PASSION

Today's Life-line

Today my PASSION is reignited in pursuit of THE GOOD LIFE.

The Good Life Application

_____

_____

_____

_____

_____

WONDERFUL WORDS OF LIFE

Day 139   May 19

The word of the day is...

PURPOSE

Today's Life-line

Today I seek to fulfill my unique PURPOSE.

The Good Life Application

_____

_____

_____

_____

_____

Day 140   May 20

The word of the day is…

COMPASSION

Today's Life-line

Today my heart overflows with COMPASSION for those who are hurting.

The Good Life Application

_____

_____

_____

_____

_____

Day 141   May 21

The word of the day is...

PROMISE

Today's Life-line

Today I will honor what I PROMISE to God, myself and others.

The Good Life Application

_____

_____

_____

_____

_____

Day 142   May 22

The word of the day is…

DOMINION

Today's Life-line

Today I yield to God's DOMINION and power.

The Good Life Application

_____

_____

_____

_____

_____

Day 143   May 23

The word of the day is…

VIRTUES

Today's Life-line

Today my life is infused with the virtues of faith, hope and love.

The Good Life Application

_____

_____

_____

_____

_____

Day 144   May 24

The word of the day is…

FAVOR

Today's Life-line

Today I am grateful for the FAVOR of God and others in my life.

The Good Life Application

_____

_____

_____

_____

_____

WONDERFUL WORDS OF LIFE

Day 145   **May 25**

The word of the day is…

UNDERSTANDING

Today's Life-line

Today I offer the gift of UNDERSTANDING.

The Good Life Application

_____

_____

_____

_____

_____

Day 146   May 26

The word of the day is…

DETERMINED

Today's Life-line

Today I am DETERMINED to live THE GOOD LIFE despite any obstacles.

The Good Life Application

_____

_____

_____

_____

_____

Day 147　　　　　　　　May 27

The word of the day is…

TOUCH

Today's Life-line

Today I TOUCH the heart of God through loving others.

The Good Life Application

_____

_____

_____

_____

_____

Day 148   **May 28**

The word of the day is…

PREPARE

Today's Life-line

Today I PREPARE my heart to give and receive more love.

The Good Life Application

_____

_____

_____

_____

_____

WONDERFUL WORDS OF LIFE

Day 149   May 29

The word of the day is…

REIGN

Today's Life-line

Today I give God all access to REIGN in my life.

The Good Life Application

_____

_____

_____

_____

_____

Day 150   May 30

The word of the day is...

REST

Today's Life-line

Today I REST to find peace and restoration.

The Good Life Application

_____

_____

_____

_____

_____

WONDERFUL WORDS OF LIFE

Day 151   May 31

The word of the day is...

CONQUEROR

Today's Life-line

Today I am more than a CONQUEROR.

The Good Life Application

_____

_____

_____

_____

_____

June

FAITHFUL

"But without faith it is impossible to please God."
Hebrews 11:16

      This is a simple statement that reveals the whole truth about living **the good life**. Faith is the key that unlocks the door to your heart's desire. If living **the good life** is rooted in pursuing your purpose then you must be faithful.

      Faith in God is the number one requirement. You must have faith that he is who he says he is and can do all things but fail. You cannot allow your faith to waiver but you must be steadfast. Faith is <u>F</u>orging <u>A</u>head <u>I</u>n <u>T</u>rusting <u>H</u>im.

      Secondly, you must have faith in your mission. You must operate according to your faith that you are engaged in *"mission possible."* You must have faith that the mission that you have been assigned to and designed for is worth it all. Faith is believing without seeing and trusting without testing.

      Thirdly, you must have faith in yourself. You must believe and have faith that you can do all things through Christ who gives us strength. You must know beyond the shadow of a doubt that you were indeed hand-picked for the mission at hand. You know that faith in yourself does not come from any greatness within yourself but rather from the Great one who called you. He trusted you enough to make a divine deposit in you to fulfill your purpose. ***"For whom he foreknew, he also predestined...Who is*** *predestined he also called, whom he called, these he also justified and whom he justified, these he also glorified." Romans 8:29-30 NIV*

Day 152   June 1

The word of the day is...

FAITHFUL

Today's Life-line

Today I am FAITHFUL in my pursuit of THE GOOD LIFE.

The Good Life Application

_____

_____

_____

_____

_____

Day 153   June 2

The word of the day is...

HAIL

Today's Life-line

Today I HAIL Christ the king as the Lord of my life.

The Good Life Application

_____

_____

_____

_____

Day 154   June 3

The word of the day is...
DISCERNMENT

Today's Life-line

Today I exercise DISCERNMENT in all of my dealings.

The Good Life Application

_____

_____

_____

_____

_____

Day 155   June 4

The word of the day is...

EXALT

Today's Life-line

Today I EXALT almighty God for the great things that he has done.

The Good Life Application

_____

_____

_____

_____

_____

WONDERFUL WORDS OF LIFE

Day 156   **June 5**

The word of the day is...

TREASURE

Today's Life-line

Today I acknowledge that my faith in God is my greatest TREASURE.

The Good Life Application

_____

_____

_____

_____

_____

Day 157   June 6

The word of the day is…
HARMONY

Today's Life-line
Today I strive for HARMONY in my relationships.

The Good Life Application

_____

_____

_____

_____

_____

WONDERFUL WORDS OF LIFE

Day 158　　　　　　June 7

The word of the day is...
APPRECIATION

Today's Life-line

Today I express APPRECIATION to God and others.

The Good Life Application

_____

_____

_____

_____

_____

Day 159   June 8

The word of the day is…
CONSECRATED

Today's Life-line

Today I take my life and let it be; CONSECRATED Lord to thee.

The Good Life Application

_____

_____

_____

_____

_____

WONDERFUL WORDS OF LIFE

Day 160   **June 9**

The word of the day is...

LEAD

Today's Life-line

Today I will follow wherever God's plan shall LEAD me.

The Good Life Application

_____

_____

_____

_____

_____

WONDERFUL WORDS OF LIFE

Day 161　　　　　　　　　June 10

The word of the day is…

REDEEMED

Today's Life-line
Today I rejoice because I am REDEEMED.

The Good Life Application

_____

_____

_____

_____

_____

WONDERFUL WORDS OF LIFE

Day 162　　　　　　　June 11

The word of the day is…
BLAMELESS

Today's Life-line

Today although I am not sinless; I am BLAMELESS because of Christ.

The Good Life Application

_____

_____

_____

_____

_____

Day 163   June 12

The word of the day is…

MERCY

Today's Life-line

Today I extend and receive MERCY.

The Good Life Application

_____

_____

_____

_____

_____

Day 164   June 13

The word of the day is…

TRUTH

Today's Life-line

Today the TRUTH shall set me free.

The Good Life Application

_____

_____

_____

_____

_____

WONDERFUL WORDS OF LIFE

Day 165   June 14

The word of the day is…

GENTLENESS

Today's Life-line

Today I approach difficult people and situations with GENTLENESS.

The Good Life Application

_____

_____

_____

_____

_____

Day 166   June 15

The word of the day is...

MEEKNESS

Today's Life-line

Today I display the fruit of the spirit MEEKNESS which is not weakness.

The Good Life Application

_____

_____

_____

_____

_____

WONDERFUL WORDS OF LIFE

Day 167　　　　　　　　June 16

The word of the day is…
KINDNESS

Today's Life-line
Today I offer my enemies the gift of KINDNESS.

The Good Life Application

_____

_____

_____

_____

_____

Day 168   June 17

The word of the day is…

UNSTUCK

Today's Life-line

Today I work toward becoming UNSTUCK.

The Good Life Application

_____

_____

_____

_____

_____

Day 169   June 18

The word of the day is…

SELFLESS

Today's Life-line
Today I strive to be SELFLESS; not selfish.

The Good Life Application

_____

_____

_____

_____

Day 170   June 19

The word of the day is…

CONFESS

Today's Life-line

Today I CONFESS my sins so that I may be an overcomer.

The Good Life Application

_____

_____

_____

_____

_____

WONDERFUL WORDS OF LIFE

Day 171　　　　　　　　June 20

The word of the day is…
CONTRIBUTE

Today's Life-line

Today I CONTRIBUTE my time, talent or resources to a worthy cause.

The Good Life Application

_____

_____

_____

_____

_____

WONDERFUL WORDS OF LIFE

Day 172   June 21

The word of the day is…

COMFORT

Today's Life-line

Today I offer COMFORT to someone who is hurting.

The Good Life Application

_____

_____

_____

_____

_____

Day 173　　　　　　　　June 22

The word of the day is…
CELEBRATE

Today's Life-line

Today I CELEBRATE the endless possibilities of THE GOOD LIFE.

The Good Life Application

_____

_____

_____

_____

_____

Day 174   June 23

The word of the day is…

EQUIPPED

Today's Life-line

Today I am EQUIPPED and ready for battle.

The Good Life Application

_____

_____

_____

_____

_____

Day 175   June 24

The word of the day is…

SHOW

Today's Life-line

Today I SHOW and share the best of myself.

The Good Life Application

_____

_____

_____

_____

Day 176   June 25

The word of the day is…

CIRCLE

Today's Life-line

Today I connect with my inner CIRCLE.

The Good Life Application

_____

_____

_____

_____

_____

WONDERFUL WORDS OF LIFE

Day 177   June 26

The word of the day is...
FELLOWSHIP

Today's Life-line

Today I seek FELLOWSHIP with those who are like minded.

The Good Life Application

_____

_____

_____

_____

_____

WONDERFUL WORDS OF LIFE

Day 178   June 27

The word of the day is...
SHELTER

Today's Life-line

Today God is my SHELTER and safety in the storms of life.

The Good Life Application

_____

_____

_____

_____

_____

Day 179   **June 28**

The word of the day is...

HEALTHY

Today's Life-line
Today I exercise HEALTHY choices.

The Good Life Application

_____

_____

_____

_____

_____

Day 180　　　　　　　　June 29

The word of the day is...
RELATIONSHIPS

Today's Life-line

Today I strengthen my RELATIONSHIPS with God and others.

The Good Life Application

_____

_____

_____

_____

_____

Day 181   June 30

The word of the day is…

GENEROUS

Today's Life-line

Today I am a blessing to others by giving with a GENEROUS heart.

The Good Life Application

_____

_____

_____

_____

_____

July

HUMBLE

"By humility and the fear of the Lord are riches, honor and life." Proverbs 22:4 KJV

In pursuit of **the good life** you must maintain a humble attitude. God requires that you do not think of yourself more highly than you ought to. When you come to the end of yourself and put on humility then you open the gateway to **the good life**.

God honors a humble spirit. When you seek to do "good" just for "goodness sake", then you reap goodness. You must acknowledge that God is really the "good" in **the good life**. It is all about him never about us. However, you reap the benefits and rewards when you humbly follow his leading.

"God resists the proud, but gives grace to the humble." 1 Peter 5:5 KJV. When you allow pride to get in the mix, you undermine your own efforts and minimize your blessings. Being humble allows God to flood you with his grace which flows freely from his endless love. It is that amazing grace that ushers you into **the good life** and sustains you.

Being humble isn't always easy because human nature craves acceptance, attention and applause. However, when you embrace humility, you set yourself up for **the good life** here and in the hereafter.

Day 182   **July 1**

The word of the day is...

HUMBLE

Today's Life-line

Today I follow the example of Christ and I HUMBLE myself.

The Good Life Application

_____

_____

_____

_____

_____

Day 183   July 2

The word of the day is...
REQUEST

Today's Life-line

Today I REQUEST that God would remove my pride and replace it with humility.

The Good Life Application

_____

_____

_____

_____

Day 184   July 3

The word of the day is…

OBEY

Today's Life-line
Today I trust and OBEY God.

The Good Life Application

_____

_____

_____

_____

_____

WONDERFUL WORDS OF LIFE

Day 185   **July 4**

The word of the day is...
BOLD

Today's Life-line

Today I am BOLD, bodacious and bound for THE GOOD LIFE.

The Good Life Application

_____

_____

_____

_____

Day 186   July 5

The word of the day is…

UPLIFT

Today's Life-line

Today I UPLIFT someone who is downtrodden.

The Good Life Application

_____

_____

_____

_____

_____

Day 187 **July 6**

The word of the day is…
CREATE

Today's Life-line

Today as I CREATE, I am an extension of the divine Creator.

The Good Life Application

_____

_____

_____

_____

_____

Day 188   July 7

The word of the day is…

REAP

Today's Life-line

Today I sow a "GOOD LIFE" seed that I may REAP a "GOOD LIFE" harvest.

The Good Life Application

_____

_____

_____

_____

_____

WONDERFUL WORDS OF LIFE

Day 189   July 8

The word of the day is...
MEDITATE

Today's Life-line
Today I MEDITATE on the promises of God.

The Good Life Application

_____

_____

_____

_____

_____

WONDERFUL WORDS OF LIFE

Day 190　　　　　　　　　July 9

The word of the day is…
ETERNAL

Today's Life-line
Today I build my hope on things ETERNAL.

The Good Life Application

_____

_____

_____

_____

_____

WONDERFUL WORDS OF LIFE

Day 191   **July 10**

The word of the day is...
STRETCH

Today's Life-line

Today I STRETCH beyond my self-imposed boundaries and limitations.

The Good Life Application

_____

_____

_____

_____

_____

Day 192　　　　　　　　July 11

The word of the day is…

BREATHE

Today's Life-line

Today as I BREATHE, I am thankful for every breath.

The Good Life Application

_____

_____

_____

_____

_____

Day 193 **July 12**

The word of the day is...
TIMING

Today's Life-line
Today I operate in God's perfect TIMING.

The Good Life Application

_____

_____

_____

_____

_____

WONDERFUL WORDS OF LIFE

Day 194   July 13

The word of the day is…

REFILL

Today's Life-line

Today I take time to rest and REFILL for the journey ahead.

The Good Life Application

_____

_____

_____

_____

_____

WONDERFUL WORDS OF LIFE

Day 195   July 14

The word of the day is…

RESIST

Today's Life-line
Today I RESIST temptation.

The Good Life Application

_____

_____

_____

_____

_____

WONDERFUL WORDS OF LIFE

Day 196   July 15

The word of the day is…

SEE

Today's Life-line

Today I SEE the B-I-G picture.

The Good Life Application

_____

_____

_____

_____

_____

WONDERFUL WORDS OF LIFE

Day 197   July 16

The word of the day is…

GROW

Today's Life-line

Today I look for areas where I need to GROW.

The Good Life Application

_____

_____

_____

_____

_____

WONDERFUL WORDS OF LIFE

Day 198   July 17

The word of the day is...

TURN

Today's Life-line

Today I TURN from things that are counterproductive to THE GOOD LIFE.

The Good Life Application

_____

_____

_____

_____

_____

WONDERFUL WORDS OF LIFE

Day 199　　　　　　　July 18

The word of the day is…
COMMUNION

Today's Life-line

Today I look for precious moments of sweet COMMUNION with God.

The Good Life Application

_____

_____

_____

_____

_____

Day 200   July 19

The word of the day is…

INCREASE

Today's Life-line

Today I decrease as I invite God to INCREASE.

The Good Life Application

_____

_____

_____

_____

_____

Day 201   July 20

The word of the day is...

BRIDGE

Today's Life-line

Today I BRIDGE the gap between where I am and where God wants me to be.

The Good Life Application

_____

_____

_____

_____

_____

WONDERFUL WORDS OF LIFE

Day 202   July 21

The word of the day is…
CONNECT

Today's Life-line

Today I CONNECT with others who are in pursuit of THE GOOD LIFE.

The Good Life Application

_____

_____

_____

_____

_____

WONDERFUL WORDS OF LIFE

Day 203   July 22

The word of the day is…

FORWARD

Today's Life-line

Today I move FORWARD, onward and upward.

The Good Life Application

_____

_____

_____

_____

_____

WONDERFUL WORDS OF LIFE

Day 204 July 23

The word of the day is…

FUN

Today's Life-line
Today I take a time-out to have FUN.

The Good Life Application

_____

_____

_____

_____

_____

Day 205   July 24

The word of the day is…

PATHWAY

Today's Life-line

Today I trust God as he leads me along the PATHWAY to my purpose.

The Good Life Application

_____

_____

_____

_____

_____

WONDERFUL WORDS OF LIFE

Day 206　　　　　　July 25

The word of the day is…
TARGET

Today's Life-line

Today I make my TARGET loving those who feel unloved.

The Good Life Application

_____
_____
_____
_____
_____

WONDERFUL WORDS OF LIFE

Day 207 July 26

The word of the day is…
SINCERE

Today's Life-line
Today I am honest and SINCERE.

The Good Life Application

_____

_____

_____

_____

WONDERFUL WORDS OF LIFE

Day 208　　　　　　　　July 27

The word of the day is…

DIVINE

Today's Life-line
Today I am open to DIVINE guidance.

The Good Life Application

_____

_____

_____

_____

_____

Day 209   July 28

The word of the day is…

EXPAND

Today's Life-line

Today I EXPAND my vision as God expands my territory.

The Good Life Application

_____

_____

_____

_____

_____

WONDERFUL WORDS OF LIFE

Day 210   July 29

The word of the day is…

EXPLORE

Today's Life-line

Today I EXPLORE new opportunities and options.

The Good Life Application

_____

_____

_____

_____

_____

WONDERFUL WORDS OF LIFE

Day 211   **July 30**

The word of the day is…
INCLUDE

Today's Life-line

Today I reach out to INCLUDE those who need more grace.

The Good Life Application

_____

_____

_____

_____

_____

WONDERFUL WORDS OF LIFE

Day 212　　　　　July 31

The word of the day is…
DECIDE

Today's Life-line

Today I DECIDE to focus on the possibilities, not the problems.

The Good Life Application

_____

_____

_____

_____

_____

August

FEARLESS

God has not given us a spirit of fear but of power, love and a sound mind. 2 Timothy 1:7

Fear has no place in **the good life**. Simply stated, fear and faith cannot co-exist. You either have one or the other. When faith is used to live **the good life,** fear is overpowered. Everyone finds themselves facing situations that can stir up fear and cause one to lose sight of the truth. But you must remind yourself that you never have to succumb to fear. The truth is you can always overcome through Christ.

God has given you power in your words, activities and interactions. You are empowered by the truth that God is always with you. He is a constant help in trouble and a supplier of every good and perfect gift. It is this very power from on high that enables you to passionately pursue the purpose for which you were created. How wonderful it is to live **the good life** without the burden of fear.

God has also given you the gift of love as an anecdote to fear. **"Perfect love cast out all fear." 1 John 4:18.** When you are washed in the Father's perfect love; you become fearless because you fear...less. No matter what challenges, obstacles, setbacks, mistakes, sins and enemies you face, you take confidence in knowing that you are covered with love, pardoned by grace and declared more than a conqueror.

God has also given you a sound mind. Though storms of confusion may rage on every side, God has equipped you with words and affirmations to keep you rooted and grounded in the truth. Living **the good life** requires right thinking, right speaking and right living. A sound mind allows God to download visions, hope and dreams that enable you to truly live **the good life**...FEARLESSLY!

"We may boldly say: The Lord is my helper; I will not fear. What can man do to me?"   Hebrews 13:6

Day 213   **August 1**

The word of the day is…
FEARLESS

Today's Life-line
Today I am FEARLESS because of my faith.

The Good Life Application

_____

_____

_____

_____

_____

WONDERFUL WORDS OF LIFE

Day 214   August 2

The word of the day is...
NEW

Today's Life-line
Today I embrace NEW and exciting possibilities.

The Good Life Application

_____

_____

_____

_____

_____

Day 215　　　　　　　August 3

The word of the day is…
DRIVEN

Today's Life-line
Today I am DRIVIEN by my purpose.

The Good Life Application

_____

_____

_____

_____

_____

WONDERFUL WORDS OF LIFE

Day 216   August 4

The word of the day is...

PRESS

Today's Life-line

Today I PRESS toward the mark of the high calling.

The Good Life Application

_____

_____

_____

_____

_____

WONDERFUL WORDS OF LIFE

Day 217   August 5

The word of the day is...

REPAIR

Today's Life-line

Today I ask God to REPAIR my broken places.

The Good Life Application

_____

_____

_____

_____

_____

Day 218   August 6

The word of the day is…
DEEP

Today's Life-line
Today I look DEEP inside to see my true self.

The Good Life Application

_____

_____

_____

_____

_____

WONDERFUL WORDS OF LIFE

Day 219   August 7

The word of the day is...

LIBERTY

Today's Life-line

Today I give myself LIBERTY to hope and dream.

The Good Life Application

_____

_____

_____

_____

_____

WONDERFUL WORDS OF LIFE

Day 220   August 8

The word of the day is…

RELY

Today's Life-line

Today I RELY solely on Godly strength, courage and wisdom.

The Good Life Application

_____

_____

_____

_____

_____

Day 221 August 9

The word of the day is…

PROSPER

Today's Life-line

Today no weapon formed against me shall PROSPER.

The Good Life Application

_____

_____

_____

_____

_____

WONDERFUL WORDS OF LIFE

Day 222   August 10

The word of the day is…
COVENANT

Today's Life-line
Today I honor my COVENANT with God.

The Good Life Application

_____

_____

_____

_____

Day 223   August 11

The word of the day is...

QUIET

Today's Life-line

Today I take time for QUIET reflection.

The Good Life Application

_____

_____

_____

_____

_____

Day 224   August 12

The word of the day is…

PLAN

Today's Life-line

Today I will follow the Master's plan while holding the Master's hand.

The Good Life Application

_____

_____

_____

_____

_____

Day 225   August 13

The word of the day is...

MEND

Today's Life-line

Today I strive to MEND broken fences.

The Good Life Application

_____

_____

_____

_____

_____

WONDERFUL WORDS OF LIFE

Day 226   August 14

The word of the day is…

GATHER

Today's Life-line

Today I GATHER only what I need for today.

The Good Life Application

_____

_____

_____

_____

_____

Day 227   August 15

The word of the day is…

ANTICIPATE

Today's Life-line

Today I ANTICIPATE the fulfillment of God's promises.

The Good Life Application

_____

_____

_____

_____

_____

Day 228   August 16

The word of the day is…

TRANSITION

Today's Life-line

Today I am in TRANSITION from the comfort zone to THE GOOD LIFE.

The Good Life Application

_____

_____

_____

_____

_____

Day 229   **August 17**

The word of the day is…

STRIVE

Today's Life-line

Today I STRIVE to do that which I am uniquely called to do.

The Good Life Application

_____

_____

_____

_____

_____

Day 230   August 18

The word of the day is...

EDIFY

Today's Life-line

Today my words EDIFY and bless the hearers.

The Good Life Application

_____

_____

_____

_____

_____

Day 231   August 19

The word of the day is...
CHOICES

Today's Life-line

Today I make CHOICES that will lead me to THE GOOD LIFE.

The Good Life Application

_____

_____

_____

_____

_____

WONDERFUL WORDS OF LIFE

Day 232 August 20

The word of the day is…

WELLNESS

Today's Life-line

Today I embrace WELLNESS and wholeness.

The Good Life Application

_____

_____

_____

_____

_____

WONDERFUL WORDS OF LIFE

Day 233   **August 21**

The word of the day is…

NEXT

Today's Life-line

Today I am ready to go to the NEXT level.

The Good Life Application

_____

_____

_____

_____

WONDERFUL WORDS OF LIFE

Day 234											August 22

The word of the day is…
STEADFAST

Today's Life-line

Today I am STEADFAST, unmovable and unshaken.

The Good Life Application

_____

_____

_____

_____

_____

Day 235   August 23

The word of the day is...

PROTECTION

Today's Life-line

Today I am covered with almighty PROTECTION.

The Good Life Application

_____

_____

_____

_____

Day 236　　　　　　　　　August 24

The word of the day is…

GREATNESS

Today's Life-line

Today I look for God to transform me from goodness to GREATNESS.

The Good Life Application

_____

_____

_____

_____

_____

WONDERFUL WORDS OF LIFE

Day 237   August 25

The word of the day is...

GUIDANCE

Today's Life-line

Today I look to the Creator for divine GUIDANCE.

The Good Life Application

_____

_____

_____

_____

Day 238   August 26

The word of the day is…

INTERCESSION

Today's Life-line

Today I make INTERCESSION through prayer for one of my enemies.

The Good Life Application

_____

_____

_____

_____

_____

WONDERFUL WORDS OF LIFE

Day 239   August 27

The word of the day is...

LISTEN

Today's Life-line

Today I LISTEN to my inner voice.

The Good Life Application

_____

_____

_____

_____

_____

Day 240　　　　　　　August 28

The word of the day is…

REMEMBER

Today's Life-line

Today I REMEMBER every valley that God brought me through.

The Good Life Application

_____

_____

_____

_____

_____

Day 241   August 29

The word of the day is…

CONFESS

Today's Life-line

Today I CONFESS my fears and insecurities.

The Good Life Application

_____

_____

_____

_____

_____

Day 242   August 30

The word of the day is…
INFLUENCE

Today's Life-line

Today my positive attitude has a positive INFLUENCE on others.

The Good Life Application

_____

_____

_____

_____

_____

Day 243   **August 31**

The word of the day is...

GUARD

Today's Life-line

Today I GUARD my heart and my spirit against negativity.

The Good Life Application

_____

_____

_____

_____

_____

WONDERFUL WORDS OF LIFE

September

PATIENCE

"After he had patiently endured, he obtained the promise."
Hebrews 6:15

Many say, "Lord give me patience and I want it now!" It may sound funny, but this is the mindset that has to change in order to live **the good life**. Too often more value is placed on the pursuit of what one desires to achieve then on the divine timing of things. If everything happens in due season, then there is no need to rush. Of course, if divine order is activated then the course of your journey navigates itself according to the master plan.

One needs to exercise patience with the Master and his plan. God is aware of every detail and every outcome. You only see glimpses but God knows the whole picture. You must trust and confidently wait on him. "Wait" is considered a 4-letter word by many and often stirs up feelings of anxiety and even resentment toward God. However, if you wait patiently on the Lord, he will renew your strength. This is not to say that things will always go the way that you expect or even want, but it will go according to the God's plan.

You must also be patient with yourself. You cannot allow external elements to dictate your course. You must be confident that as you pursue **the good life**, you will have, do and be what you need. Surely mistakes will be made along the journey, but we must patiently endure the lessons that will yield the desired fruit. As we are all perfectly imperfect we must allow for room to grow and the time that it takes to get to the "good life".

We must also be patient with the process. All things truly work together for good and you must be willing to wait for the manifestation. Each piece of the puzzle must be rightly fit together and that process takes time. As you wait it out, God is working out magnificent pathways to **the good life**. As you pursue your purpose you must be open to God's will in God's way...in God's perfect timing.

"Wait on the Lord, be of good courage, and he shall strengthen your heart; wait I say on the Lord." Psalm 27: 14

Day 244　　　　　　　　September 1

The word of the day is…
PATIENCE

Today's Life-line
Today I exercise PATIENCE in all situations.

The Good Life Application

_____

_____

_____

_____

_____

WONDERFUL WORDS OF LIFE

Day 245 September 2

The word of the day is...
ANOINTED

Today's Life-line

Today I do the work that God has ANOINTED me to do.

The Good Life Application

_____

_____

_____

_____

_____

WONDERFUL WORDS OF LIFE

Day 246 September 3

The word of the day is…

APPOINTED

Today's Life-line

Today I do the work that God has APPOINTED me to do.

The Good Life Application

_____

_____

_____

_____

_____

Day 247   **September 4**

The word of the day is…

ASSIGNMENT

Today's Life-line

Today I accept the ASSIGNMENT that God created me to fulfill.

The Good Life Application

_____

_____

_____

_____

_____

Day 248   **September 5**

The word of the day is…
SEASON

Today's Life-line
Today I embrace this SEASON of my life.

The Good Life Application

_____

_____

_____

_____

_____

WONDERFUL WORDS OF LIFE

Day 249 September 6

The word of the day is…
ABUNDANCE

Today's Life-line
Today I am blessed with God's ABUNDANCE.

The Good Life Application

_____

_____

_____

_____

Day 250　　　　　September 7

The word of the day is…

FRIEND

Today's Life-line
Today I open my heart to a FRIEND.

The Good Life Application

_____

_____

_____

_____

_____

WONDERFUL WORDS OF LIFE

Day 251   **September 8**

The word of the day is...

OVERFLOW

Today's Life-line

Today I bless someone else from my OVERFLOW.

The Good Life Application

_____

_____

_____

_____

_____

WONDERFUL WORDS OF LIFE

Day 252 　　　　　**September 9**

The word of the day is...

TRUTH

Today's Life-line

Today I lovingly speak the TRUTH to myself and others.

The Good Life Application

_____

_____

_____

_____

_____

WONDERFUL WORDS OF LIFE

Day 253   September 10

The word of the day is…

DIRECTION

Today's Life-line

Today I move in the DIRECTION of THE GOOD LIFE.

The Good Life Application

_____

_____

_____

_____

WONDERFUL WORDS OF LIFE

Day 254 September 11

The word of the day is…

REWARD

Today's Life-line

Today as I deal with earthly challenges, I work for a heavenly REWARD.

The Good Life Application

_____

_____

_____

_____

_____

Day 255   **September 12**

The word of the day is...
SEARCH

Today's Life-line

Today I SEARCH my heart and ask God to purge my impurities.

The Good Life Application

_____

_____

_____

_____

_____

WONDERFUL WORDS OF LIFE

Day 256　　　　　　September 13

The word of the day is…

CAN

Today's Life-line

Today I CAN and will do all things through Christ who gives me strength.

The Good Life Application

_____

_____

_____

_____

_____

Day 257   **September 14**

The word of the day is...
SMILE

Today's Life-line
Today my SMILE will reflect God's light and love.

The Good Life Application

_____

_____

_____

_____

_____

WONDERFUL WORDS OF LIFE

Day 258   September 15

The word of the day is...
PERSPECTIVE

Today's Life-line
Today I adjust my PERSPECTIVE.

The Good Life Application

_____

_____

_____

_____

_____

Day 259   September 16

The word of the day is…

CLOSER

Today's Life-line

Today I am one step CLOSER to living THE GOOD LIFE.

The Good Life Application

_____

_____

_____

_____

_____

WONDERFUL WORDS OF LIFE

Day 260　　　　September 17

The word of the day is…

PUSH

Today's Life-line

Today I PUSH just a little harder toward my goals.

The Good Life Application

_____

_____

_____

_____

_____

Day 261   September 18

The word of the day is…

PAUSE

Today's Life-line
Today I PAUSE just to say thank you.

The Good Life Application

_____

_____

_____

_____

WONDERFUL WORDS OF LIFE

Day 262   September 19

The word of the day is…

AVAILABLE

Today's Life-line

Today I am AVAILABLE to God, my creator.

The Good Life Application

_____

_____

_____

_____

_____

Day 263　　　　　　September 20

The word of the day is…
EFFORT

Today's Life-line

Today I make more of an EFFORT to serve God and others.

The Good Life Application

_____

_____

_____

_____

_____

WONDERFUL WORDS OF LIFE

Day 264　　　　September 21

The word of the day is…

LEGACY

Today's Life-line

Today I live my life such that I leave a LEGACY of faith.

The Good Life Application

_____

_____

_____

_____

_____

WONDERFUL WORDS OF LIFE

Day 265 **September 22**

The word of the day is…
CHASE

Today's Life-line

Today I CHASE after that which will lead me to THE GOOD LIFE.

The Good Life Application

_____

_____

_____

_____

Day 266   September 23

The word of the day is...

AUTHENTIC

Today's Life-line

Today I am AUTHENTIC in my relationships.

The Good Life Application

_____

_____

_____

_____

_____

WONDERFUL WORDS OF LIFE

Day 267   September 24

The word of the day is…
FORTIFIED

Today's Life-line
Today I am FORTIFIED with power from on high.

The Good Life Application

_____

_____

_____

_____

_____

WONDERFUL WORDS OF LIFE

Day 268   **September 25**

The word of the day is…

CLARITY

Today's Life-line

Today my vision has CLARITY.

The Good Life Application

_____

_____

_____

_____

_____

WONDERFUL WORDS OF LIFE

Day 269   **September 26**

The word of the day is...
HAPPINESS

Today's Life-line

Today I choose HAPPINESS regardless of my circumstance.

The Good Life Application

_____

_____

_____

_____

_____

WONDERFUL WORDS OF LIFE

Day 270　　　　　September 27

The word of the day is...

BEAUTIFUL

Today's Life-line

Today I acknowledge that I am one of God's BEAUTIFUL creations.

The Good Life Application

_____

_____

_____

_____

_____

Day 271   September 28

The word of the day is...
CLOSE

Today's Life-line
Today I draw CLOSE to God and those that I love.

The Good Life Application

_____

_____

_____

_____

_____

Day 272 September 29

The word of the day is…

VICTORY

Today's Life-line
Today I claim VICTORY over adversity.

The Good Life Application

_____

_____

_____

_____

_____

Day 273   **September 30**

The word of the day is…
ALL

Today's Life-line
Today I surrender ALL.

The Good Life Application

_____

_____

_____

_____

_____

October

FOCUS

"Do you know that in a race all the runners run, but only one gets the prize? Run in such a way as to get the prize. Everyone who competes in the games goes into strict training. They do it to get a crown that will last forever." 1 Corinthians 9:24, 25 NIV

Focus is essential for living **the good life**. In a world full of distractions and attractions it is easy to get derailed on the path to **the good life**. In order for you to accomplish what you want you must be focused. By keeping your eyes on the prize you are able to run the race with fortitude. As you move forward, you must be persistent, consistent and resistant. When you are consistent you continue to work at the same level of fervor, maintaining your passion for the purpose. When you are persistent you do not allow the pitfalls to impede your progress. When you are resistant you ignore the attempts of the enemy to convince you that you are destined for failure. You indeed remain unstoppable, unchangeable, unbreakable and unshakeable in your pursuit of your calling.

Ten keys to help you stay focused:

1. **Pray** individually and collectively with a partner or group.
2. **Read** the Bible and other inspirational materials.
3. **Fast** to deny some area of self-indulgence which will develop discipline.
4. **Eliminate** or minimize distractions.

5. **Create** a vision or possibility board to keep your eye on the prize.
6. **Connect** with likeminded people who are in pursuit of the "good life".
7. **Recite** affirmations to reinforce your goals.
8. **Write** in a journal about your journey.
9. **Listen** to inspirational music and teachings.
10. **Remind** yourself of past successes.

When you are focused you can endure and withstand any opposition. Be aware that others are watching you run the race and will bear witness when you receive the prize of **the good life**. With faith, focus and follow through you will surely get the prize!

Day 274   October 1

The word of the day is…

FOCUS

Today's Life-line

Today I keep my FOCUS only on the main thing.

The Good Life Application

_____

_____

_____

_____

_____

Day 275   October 2

The word of the day is…

MANIFEST

Today's Life-line

Today I rejoice as I see God's plan MANIFEST in my life.

The Good Life Application

_____

_____

_____

_____

_____

WONDERFUL WORDS OF LIFE

Day 276　　　　　　　　October 3

The word of the day is…

ACCESS

Today's Life-line

Today I ACCESS my inner strength.

The Good Life Application

_____

_____

_____

_____

_____

Day 277　　　　　　October 4

The word of the day is…
IMAGINE

Today's Life-line

Today I IMAGINE the goodness of living THE GOOD LIFE.

The Good Life Application

_____

_____

_____

_____

_____

Day 278   October 5

The word of the day is…

ADVANCE

Today's Life-line

Today I ADVANCE towards life that God intends for me to live.

The Good Life Application

_____

_____

_____

_____

_____

Day 279   October 6

The word of the day is...
RESULTS

Today's Life-line

Today I focus on positive RESULTS from my positive actions.

The Good Life Application

_____

_____

_____

_____

_____

Day 280　　　　　　　　October 7

The word of the day is…
PROCLAIM

Today's Life-line
Today I PROCLAIM that I am an overcomer.

The Good Life Application

_____

_____

_____

_____

_____

Day 281　　　　　　October 8

The word of the day is…

MANY

Today's Life-line

Today I count my MANY blessings.

The Good Life Application

_____

_____

_____

_____

_____

WONDERFUL WORDS OF LIFE

Day 282   October 9

The word of the day is...

HELP

Today's Life-line

Today I look to God to HELP me live THE GOOD LIFE.

The Good Life Application

_____

_____

_____

_____

_____

Day 283   October 10

The word of the day is...
REPLENISH

Today's Life-line

Today I look to God to REPLENISH my strength for the journey.

The Good Life Application

_____

_____

_____

_____

_____

WONDERFUL WORDS OF LIFE

Day 284   October 11

The word of the day is…

RETREAT

Today's Life-line

Today I RETREAT to my quiet place where I find God.

The Good Life Application

_____

_____

_____

_____

_____

Day 285   **October 12**

The word of the day is...

TODAY

Today's Life-line

Today I am only concerned with TODAY.

The Good Life Application

_____

_____

_____

_____

_____

Day 286   October 13

The word of the day is...

REPOSITION

Today's Life-line

Today I REPOSITION myself to align with God's plan for me.

The Good Life Application

_____

_____

_____

_____

_____

WONDERFUL WORDS OF LIFE

Day 287   **October 14**

The word of the day is...
TEAM

Today's Life-line

Today I look for encouragement from my support TEAM.

The Good Life Application

_____

_____

_____

_____

_____

Day 288   October 15

The word of the day is…

ANSWER

Today's Life-line

Today I seek Godly wisdom and knowledge for the ANSWER.

The Good Life Application

_____

_____

_____

_____

_____

Day 289 October 16

The word of the day is…

FEED

Today's Life-line

Today I FEED my soul with the things that inspire me.

The Good Life Application

_____

_____

_____

_____

_____

WONDERFUL WORDS OF LIFE

Day 290   October 17

The word of the day is...
UNCOMPROMISED

Today's Life-line
Today I remain UNCOMPROMISED in my convictions.

The Good Life Application

_____

_____

_____

_____

_____

WONDERFUL WORDS OF LIFE

Day 291   October 18

The word of the day is…

FUTURE

Today's Life-line

Today I put in the work that will yield a brighter FUTURE.

The Good Life Application

_____

_____

_____

_____

_____

WONDERFUL WORDS OF LIFE

Day 292   October 19

The word of the day is...

RADICAL

Today's Life-line

Today my RADICAL thoughts and actions produce profound, positive change.

The Good Life Application

_____

_____

_____

_____

_____

Day 293 — October 20

The word of the day is…

UNBROKEN

Today's Life-line

Today my spirit remains UNBROKEN.

The Good Life Application

_____

_____

_____

_____

_____

Day 294　　　　　　　　　October 21

The word of the day is…
CELEBRATE

Today's Life-line
Today I CELEBRATE the gift of my GOOD LIFE.

The Good Life Application

_____

_____

_____

_____

WONDERFUL WORDS OF LIFE

Day 295   **October 22**

The word of the day is…

KINGDOM

Today's Life-line

Today I pursue KINGDOM connections.

The Good Life Application

_____

_____

_____

_____

_____

WONDERFUL WORDS OF LIFE

Day 296   October 23

The word of the day is...

CO-EXIST

Today's Life-line

Today I lovingly CO-EXIST with those who are different.

The Good Life Application

_____

_____

_____

_____

_____

WONDERFUL WORDS OF LIFE

Day 297 October 24

The word of the day is...
ONENESS

Today's Life-line
Today I surrender my will to ONENESS with God.

The Good Life Application

_____

_____

_____

_____

WONDERFUL WORDS OF LIFE

Day 298   October 25

The word of the day is…
ACTIVATE

Today's Life-line
Today I ACTIVATE my faith in God and myself.

The Good Life Application

_____

_____

_____

_____

_____

Day 299　　　　　　　　October 26

The word of the day is…
RADIATE

Today's Life-line
Today I RADIATE God's abounding love.

The Good Life Application

_____

_____

_____

_____

_____

WONDERFUL WORDS OF LIFE

Day 300   October 27

The word of the day is...

STEADY

Today's Life-line

Today I am consistent and STEADY as I press toward my goal.

The Good Life Application

_____

_____

_____

_____

_____

Day 301　　　　　　　　　October 28

The word of the day is...
DISCIPLINE

Today's Life-line

Today I exercise DISCIPLINE over my thoughts, actions and emotions.

The Good Life Application

_____

_____

_____

_____

_____

WONDERFUL WORDS OF LIFE

Day 302   October 29

The word of the day is...
ENTHUSIASM

Today's Life-line

Today my ENTHUSIASM for THE GOOD LIFE is contagious.

The Good Life Application

_____

_____

_____

_____

_____

Day 303	October 30

The word of the day is...
DETERMINED

Today's Life-line
Today I am DETERMINED to be an overcomer.

The Good Life Application

_____

_____

_____

_____

WONDERFUL WORDS OF LIFE

Day 304											October 31

The word of the day is…

QUIETNESS

Today's Life-line

Today I embrace sweet moments of QUIETNESS where I can hear God.

The Good Life Application

_____

_____

_____

_____

_____

WONDERFUL WORDS OF LIFE

November

THANKFUL

"In everything give thanks: for this is the will of God in Christ Jesus concerning you." 1 Thessalonians 5:18 KJV

"Thank you!" These are two simple words that pack a powerful punch. In order to live **the good life** you must have a thankful heart that overflows with expressions of gratitude. An attitude of gratitude extended toward God and others assures you of even greater blessings.

It is no secret that a thankful heart is fertile ground for God to plant seeds of purpose that will surely lead to **the good life**. Since **the good life** is built on purpose, power and passion, then praise and thanksgiving must also be a part of the mountain moving formula. Simply put, when praises go up, blessings rain down.

Have you ever experienced giving a special gift to someone and they are less than enthusiastic about it? You may receive a gratuitous "thank you" but it's not truly heartfelt. As a result, you feel unappreciated and unmotivated to give them a gift in the future. Conversely, when you give a gift that is welcomed and you receive a genuine, heartfelt "thank you", it motivates you to give more. So it is with the gifts that God bestows upon you. Your praise and thanksgiving motivate God to bless you abundantly with gifts... *"and then some"*.

The *"and then some"* is the extra that you receive because you have a thankful heart. A thankful heart is also a humble heart that is keenly aware of God's blessings and benefits. When you show God that you are truly grateful not just for what he has done but for who he is, then you open the gateway to **the good life**.

We are encouraged in the Bible to give thanks *"in all things"* not necessarily for all things but in all things. Although it may not feel good at the time, you must remember that God is working behind the scenes to make it "all good". **The good life** is often a mixture of rain and sunshine, but you must be thankful that it is all working together for your good. Even when your circumstances are clouded with trials, tribulations and testing; thanksgiving is the key to your breakthrough. When you focus on the good which comes from God then you are sure to receive "all of his benefits."

Praise the Lord oh my soul and forget not all his benefits. Psalm 103:2 NIV

Day 305   **November 1**

The word of the day is…
THANKFUL

Today's Life-line
Today I am THANKFUL.

The Good Life Application

_____

_____

_____

_____

_____

WONDERFUL WORDS OF LIFE

Day 306   November 2

The word of the day is...
DECREE

Today's Life-line
Today I DECREE that I will reach my goals.

The Good Life Application

_____

_____

_____

_____

_____

WONDERFUL WORDS OF LIFE

Day 307   November 3

The word of the day is…
DELIGHT

Today's Life-line

Today I DELIGHT in all of the possibilities of THE GOOD LIFE.

The Good Life Application

_____

_____

_____

_____

_____

WONDERFUL WORDS OF LIFE

Day 308 November 4

The word of the day is…

PONDER

Today's Life-line

Today I PONDER the good things and good people God has placed in my life.

The Good Life Application

_____

_____

_____

_____

_____

Day 309 **November 5**

The word of the day is...
SEEK

Today's Life-line
Today I SEEK understanding in my relationships.

The Good Life Application

_____

_____

_____

_____

_____

WONDERFUL WORDS OF LIFE

Day 310   November 6

The word of the day is…

GLORY

Today's Life-line

Today I give God the GLORY for my victory story.

The Good Life Application

_____

_____

_____

_____

_____

WONDERFUL WORDS OF LIFE

Day 311　　　　　　November 7

The word of the day is…
GROUNDED

Today's Life-line
Today I remain rooted and GROUNDED in love.

The Good Life Application

_____

_____

_____

_____

_____

Day 312   November 8

The word of the day is...
CONSECRATED

Today's Life-line
Today my life is CONSECRATED for divine works.

The Good Life Application

_____

_____

_____

_____

_____

Day 313 November 9

The word of the day is…
MOTIVATED

Today's Life-line
Today I am MOTIVATED to be my best self.

The Good Life Application

_____

_____

_____

_____

Day 314 November 10

The word of the day is…

REBUKE

Today's Life-line

Today I REBUKE the adversary's attempts to block THE GOOD LIFE.

The Good Life Application

_____

_____

_____

_____

_____

Day 315   November 11

The word of the day is…
HEALING

Today's Life-line

Today I claim physical, emotional, mental and spiritual HEALING.

The Good Life Application

_____

_____

_____

_____

_____

WONDERFUL WORDS OF LIFE

Day 316   November 12

The word of the day is…

FIXED

Today's Life-line

Today my mind is FIXED on progress and success.

The Good Life Application

_____

_____

_____

_____

_____

Day 317   November 13

The word of the day is…
TRIUMPHANT

Today's Life-line
Today I am TRIUMPHANT.

The Good Life Application

_____

_____

_____

_____

WONDERFUL WORDS OF LIFE

Day 318 November 14

The word of the day is...

MIGHTY

Today's Life-line

Today I rely on God's MIGHTY power to fight my battles.

The Good Life Application

_____

_____

_____

_____

_____

Day 319   November 15

The word of the day is…

AGREEMENT

Today's Life-line

Today I stand in AGREEMENT with a friend who needs support.

The Good Life Application

_____

_____

_____

_____

Day 320   **November 16**

The word of the day is…

REVIVAL

Today's Life-line
Today I stir up a REVIVAL in my spirit.

The Good Life Application

_____

_____

_____

_____

_____

Day 321   November 17

The word of the day is…

PRIORITIZE

Today's Life-line

Today I PRIORITIZE my life goals so that I will be victorious.

The Good Life Application

_____

_____

_____

_____

_____

WONDERFUL WORDS OF LIFE

Day 322　　　　　　　November 18

The word of the day is…

UPRIGHT

Today's Life-line

Today I walk UPRIGHT on my path to THE GOOD LIFE.

The Good Life Application

_____

_____

_____

_____

_____

Day 323 — November 19

The word of the day is…

LIMITLESS

Today's Life-line

Today I recognize that God's love, blessings and power are LIMITLESS.

The Good Life Application

_____

_____

_____

_____

_____

WONDERFUL WORDS OF LIFE

Day 324							November 20

The word of the day is…
UNITE

Today's Life-line
Today I UNITE with those who are like-minded.

The Good Life Application

_____

_____

_____

_____

_____

WONDERFUL WORDS OF LIFE

Day 325   **November 21**

The word of the day is...

LABOR

Today's Life-line
Today I LABOR not in vain.

The Good Life Application

_____

_____

_____

_____

_____

WONDERFUL WORDS OF LIFE

Day 326   November 22

The word of the day is...
TRANSFORMATION

Today's Life-line

Today I put in the work to bring about the desired TRANSFORMATION.

The Good Life Application

_____

_____

_____

_____

_____

WONDERFUL WORDS OF LIFE

Day 327   November 23

The word of the day is…

REVERANCE

Today's Life-line

Today I give REVERENCE to the things of God.

The Good Life Application

_____

_____

_____

_____

_____

WONDERFUL WORDS OF LIFE

Day 328   November 24

The word of the day is…

WITHSTAND

Today's Life-line

Today I WITHSTAND the fiery darts and doubts of opposition.

The Good Life Application

_____

_____

_____

_____

_____

Day 329 November 25

The word of the day is…
STILLNESS

Today's Life-line

Today I find strength in the quiet STILLNESS of the day.

The Good Life Application

_____

_____

_____

_____

_____

WONDERFUL WORDS OF LIFE

Day 330 November 26

The word of the day is...

RENOUNCE

Today's Life-line

Today I RENOUNCE all negative thoughts and emotions.

The Good Life Application

_____

_____

_____

_____

_____

Day 331   **November 27**

The word of the day is...
FAVOR

Today's Life-line
Today I walk in the FAVOR of God and others.

The Good Life Application

_____

_____

_____

_____

_____

WONDERFUL WORDS OF LIFE

Day 332　　　　　November 28

The word of the day is…
RESTORED

Today's Life-line
Today I praise God that I am RESTORED.

The Good Life Application

_____

_____

_____

_____

_____

WONDERFUL WORDS OF LIFE

Day 333   **November 29**

The word of the day is...
OPEN

Today's Life-line

Today I use my faith as the key to OPEN the door to THE GOOD LIFE.

The Good Life Application

_____

_____

_____

_____

_____

WONDERFUL WORDS OF LIFE

Day 334　　　　　　November 30

The word of the day is…
EASY

Today's Life-line
Today I choose to take it cool and EASY.

The Good Life Application

_____

_____

_____

_____

_____

December

FREE

"It is for freedom that Christ has set us free. Stand firm, then, and do not let yourselves be burdened again by a yoke of slavery." Galatians 5:1 NIV

FREE to **love**...*FREE* to **live**...*FREE* to **serve**...*FREE* to **give**...*FREE* to **trust**...*FREE* to **have**...*FREE* to **bear fruit**...*FREE* to **choose**...*FREE* to **win**...*FREE* to **lose**...*FREE* to **go**...*FREE* to **stay**...*FREE* to **laugh**...*FREE* to **cry**...*FREE* to **heal**...*FREE* to **release**...*FREE* to **increase**...*FREE* to **climb**...*FREE* to **arise**...*FREE* to **sing**...*FREE* to **dance**...FREE to **retreat**...*FREE* to **advance**...*FREE* to **believe**...*FREE* to **receive**...*FREE* to **embrace**...*FREE* to **relate**...*FREE* to **dream**...*FREE* to **be**_____.

"So if the son sets you free, you will be free indeed."

John 8:36 NIV

To live **the good life** is to be **FREE!** God does not want you to live in bondage to limitations. You were created as an extension of the Father's love and released into the world to fulfill your purpose. God desires for you to live **the good life** and enjoy all of its benefits. When you free yourself, you open up the gateway for the blessings to flow.

The keys to being free are:

F-Forget about the past. The only thing yesterday holds for you are the lessons learned. Don't be a prisoner of the past, press on. Each day is a new opportunity to pursue **the good life.** When we ask for forgiveness, God does not hold your pass against you. So leave those things behind and live in the now. For now is the appointed time.

WONDERFUL WORDS OF LIFE

"But one thing I do, forgetting what is behind and reaching to those things which are ahead." Philippians 3:13

R-Release yourself. Do not allow yourself to be in bondage any longer. You become free by letting go of anger, resentment, fear, unforgiveness, evil thoughts and negative words. When you shake off those chains that bind you, you free yourself to fulfill your destiny. Too often people lack fulfillment because they choose to live with self-hatred, self-inflicted punishment and self-doubt. When you release these negative things then your heart and mind can be free to live **the good life**.

"I have come that you might have life and have it more abundantly." John 10:10

E-Express yourself. Every member of "the body" has its own unique function and position. God knows why he created you just the way you are. You are perfectly designed for your assignment. It is so wonderful to think that before God created the world, he considered your piece of the puzzle. Too often you can get caught up trying to do or be like others instead of expressing yourself. You were uniquely created for your purpose and you must use your gifts and talents to accomplish it. So if you truly want to live **the good life** you must breakout, break forth, breakthrough and express yourself!

"Having then gifts differing according to the grace that is given to us, let us use them." Romans 12:6

E-Embrace your calling. *"For those he predestined he also called."* **Romans 8:29** If God has called you to a thing he will surely see you through a thing. Do not be afraid to step into that divine calling. He knows what he created you to do and *"He who began a good work in you shall continue until the*

day of Christ." Philippians 1:6 There are no mistakes in the "master plan". Trust God to lead you on the right pathway and trust him with the outcome. You must passionately pursue your calling. It is not enough to simply say it, you must live, do it and be it. ***The good life*** is achieved when you grab hold of what you were created to do. When you open yourself to embrace your calling, you will find joy and peace. When you fully embrace your divine calling ***the good life*** possibilities are endless.

"We are his workmanship created in Christ Jesus for good works, which God prepared beforehand that we should walk in them." Ephesians 2: 10

Day 335   **December 1**

The word of the day is…

FREE

Today's Life-line

Today I am FREE to be me…and the world will adjust.

The Good Life Application

_____

_____

_____

_____

_____

Day 336   December 2

The word of the day is...

CALM

Today's Life-line

Today I remain CALM in all situations.

The Good Life Application

_____

_____

_____

_____

_____

WONDERFUL WORDS OF LIFE

Day 337   December 3

The word of the day is…
NAVIGATE

Today's Life-line

Today I NAVIGATE my life according to God's plan.

The Good Life Application

_____

_____

_____

_____

_____

WONDERFUL WORDS OF LIFE

Day 338   **December 4**

The word of the day is...

CLIMB

Today's Life-line

Today I CLIMB the ladder of success without stepping on the toes of others.

The Good Life Application

_____

_____

_____

_____

_____

WONDERFUL WORDS OF LIFE

Day 339   December 5

The word of the day is…

FILLED

Today's Life-line

Today I am FILLED with the fruit of the spirit.

The Good Life Application

_____

_____

_____

_____

_____

Day 340   **December 6**

The word of the day is...
GLADNESS

Today's Life-line
Today I face each challenge with GLADNESS.

The Good Life Application

_____

_____

_____

_____

_____

WONDERFUL WORDS OF LIFE

Day 341   December 7

The word of the day is…

SURRENDER

Today's Life-line

Today I SURRENDER my thoughts, emotions and actions to God.

The Good Life Application

_____

_____

_____

_____

_____

WONDERFUL WORDS OF LIFE

Day 342   **December 8**

The word of the day is...
IMPACT

Today's Life-line

Today I am intentional about making a positive IMPACT.

The Good Life Application

_____

_____

_____

_____

_____

WONDERFUL WORDS OF LIFE

Day 343   December 9

The word of the day is...

REAL

Today's Life-line

Today I am REAL with God, myself and others.

The Good Life Application

_____

_____

_____

_____

_____

Day 344   **December 10**

The word of the day is...
ONE

Today's Life-line

Today I focus on ONE thing that will lead me to THE GOOD LIFE.

The Good Life Application

_____

_____

_____

_____

_____

WONDERFUL WORDS OF LIFE

Day 345   December 11

The word of the day is...

GRATITUDE

Today's Life-line

Today I express GRATITUDE to God and others.

The Good Life Application

_____

_____

_____

_____

_____

Day 346   December 12

The word of the day is…

Plan

Today's Life-line

Today I PLAN my work and work my PLAN.

The Good Life Application

_____

_____

_____

_____

_____

WONDERFUL WORDS OF LIFE

Day 347   December 13

The word of the day is…
DECLARE

Today's Life-line

Today I DECLARE that I will live THE GOOD LIFE that I was created to live.

The Good Life Application

_____

_____

_____

_____

_____

Day 348 **December 14**

The word of the day is...
DEPOSIT

Today's Life-line

Today I DEPOSIT positive energy into the lives of those around me.

The Good Life Application

_____

_____

_____

_____

_____

Day 349   December 15

The word of the day is…

BROKENESS

Today's Life-line

Today I offer my BROKENESS to God for mending.

The Good Life Application

_____

_____

_____

_____

_____

WONDERFUL WORDS OF LIFE

Day 350   **December 16**

The word of the day is...
CONFORM

Today's Life-line

Today I will not CONFORM to the ways of the world.

The Good Life Application

_____

_____

_____

_____

_____

WONDERFUL WORDS OF LIFE

Day 351　　　　　　December 17

The word of the day is…

INVESTIGATE

Today's Life-line

Today I INVESTIGATE before I invest my time, talent and resources.

The Good Life Application

_____

_____

_____

_____

_____

WONDERFUL WORDS OF LIFE

Day 352   **December 18**

The word of the day is...
INTERACT

Today's Life-line

Today I engage and INTERACT positively with others.

The Good Life Application

_____

_____

_____

_____

_____

WONDERFUL WORDS OF LIFE

Day 353　　December 19

The word of the day is...

OWN

Today's Life-line

Today I unashamedly OWN my truth.

The Good Life Application

_____

_____

_____

_____

_____

Day 354   **December 20**

The word of the day is...

KINDNESS

Today's Life-line

Today I make an extra effort to sow seeds of KINDNESS.

The Good Life Application

_____

_____

_____

_____

_____

Day 355   December 21

The word of the day is…

SELF-CONTROL

Today's Life-line

Today I exercise SELF-CONTROL in all areas of my life.

The Good Life Application

_____

_____

_____

_____

_____

Day 356   December 22

The word of the day is…

UNCONDITIONAL

Today's Life-line

Today I am thankful for God's UNCONDITIONAL love.

The Good Life Application

_____

_____

_____

_____

_____

WONDERFUL WORDS OF LIFE

Day 357   December 23

The word of the day is...

ACTION

Today's Life-line

Today I take ACTION in an area that challenges me.

The Good Life Application

_____

_____

_____

_____

_____

Day 358 **December 24**

The word of the day is…
FAMILY

Today's Life-line
Today I cherish my FAMILY.

The Good Life Application

_____

_____

_____

_____

_____

WONDERFUL WORDS OF LIFE

Day 359　　　　　December 25

The word of the day is…
MIRACLE

Today's Life-line

Today I rejoice in the miracle of the birth of our savior, Jesus Christ.

The Good Life Application

_____

_____

_____

_____

_____

WONDERFUL WORDS OF LIFE

Day 360   December 26

The word of the day is...

FRIENDSHIP

Today's Life-line

Today I am thankful for the gift of FRIENDSHIP.

The Good Life Application

_____

_____

_____

_____

Day 361   December 27

The word of the day is...
DETERMINATION

Today's Life-line
Today my DETERMINATION will see me through.

The Good Life Application

_____

_____

_____

_____

WONDERFUL WORDS OF LIFE

Day 362   December 28

The word of the day is…

HONOR

Today's Life-line

Today I HONOR my word.

The Good Life Application

_____

_____

_____

_____

_____

WONDERFUL WORDS OF LIFE

Day 363   December 29

The word of the day is...

EXPECTATION

Today's Life-line

Today I look ahead with great EXPECTATION for all THE GOOD LIFE has to offer.

The Good Life Application

_____

_____

_____

_____

Day 364　　　　　　December 30

The word of the day is…
PLAY

Today's Life-line
Today I give myself permission to PLAY.

The Good Life Application

_____

_____

_____

_____

_____

WONDERFUL WORDS OF LIFE

Day 365   December 31

The word of the day is…
COMPLETE

Today's Life-line

Today as I COMPLETE this year, I am excited about THE GOOD LIFE that my future holds.

The Good Life Application

_____

_____

_____

_____

_____

WONDERFUL WORDS OF LIFE

Appendix A

      For me, living THE GOOD LIFE has been based on having a personal relationship with Jesus Christ. It is not enough to know of him, but one must know and trust him as a personal savior.

What does this mean? It means that you realize that in this life you will make mistakes and bad choices that manifest as sin. You acknowledge that your sins are leading you down the path of destruction to hell. You believe that the Lord Jesus Christ died on the cross and rose again from the dead, for you sins. You accept this truth; you confess your sins to God and ask him to forgive you as you commit to living a life that is pleasing unto him. This will not only put you on track for THE GOOD LIFE now, but for eternity.

"If you confess with your mouth that Jesus is Lord and believe in your heart that God raised him from the dead, you will be saved." **Romans 10:9**

WONDERFUL WORDS OF LIFE

Made in the USA
Columbia, SC
13 January 2022